1784

THE BATTLE OF MUDEFORD

Michael F. Powell

Natula Publications

ISBN 1 897 887 01 9

Natula Publications
Briar Park Business Centre
11 Stour Road
Christchurch
Dorset
BH23 1PL

Cover illustration by Peter Newman from a design by Mike Powell.

British Library Cataloguing-in-Publication Data.
A catalogue record for this book is available from the British Library.

Printed by Pardy & Son Printers Ltd, Ringwood, Hampshire.

Contents

Illustrations

Dedication

To Margaret, Alex and Bryony

and

D.M.

William Allen,

Late Master of H.M. Sloop-of-War *Orestes*

Acknowledgements

I am grateful to the staffs of the Public Record Office at Kew and Chancery Lane, the Reading Room of the National Maritime Museum, Dorset and the Isle of Wight Record Offices, the Curators and staff of the Cowes Maritime Museum and the Red House Museum, Christchurch.

I would also like to thank my wife, Margaret and children for not only helping to type the manuscript but also putting-up with having all the earlier versions read to them. They have stood the consequences of my late hours and extended research with great fortitude.

Whilst I have taken cognisance of the advice offered by others, any errors or omissions remain mine.

Smuggling

Smuggling, in spite of its present day associations, holds a fascination for many people. Ignoring modern practices, they dream of the simpler world of two centuries ago. In this world gallant men, and a few beautiful women, risked their liberty, and maybe their lives, to import the exotic luxuries of life, running the gauntlet of avaricious Revenue men, cheating overbearing authority with a swagger and a smile.

There are hundreds of smuggling stories. This part of the coast, western Hampshire shading into Dorset with its proximity to France and the Channel Islands, has its fair share. Stories repeated frequently enough acquire credibility and often become a part of folklore. Their characters become folk heroes and the elements of truth, where they exist at all, become distorted and intertwined with myth to a point where they may no longer be separated. Many, regretably perhaps, are pure fantasy.

The facts of smuggling in the Eighteenth and early Nineteenth centuries are not really the subject of romance, nor is the background which made it such a large scale element of trade. In the days before the introduction of Income Tax in 1792, the Government had to raise money by other means, usually by levies on imports and exports or on domestic production. One of the reasons that this country did not suffer the revolutionary fervour of some parts of Europe at the end of the Eighteenth century was because these taxes were largely seen as being fair. They were rarely excessive on essential products. On luxuries, though, they were often very high indeed. Definitions of "luxury goods" vary from age to age. At this period they included wine and spirits, tea, silk, lace, jewellery and over fourteen hundred other products. In some cases the duty was six or more times the value of the goods reckoned by the cost of production, distribution and profit. If the duty were avoided, the profit could be inflated and the product still sold at well below the "legal" price.

Duty on goods produced and sold within the country was known as Excise, whilst duty on imports was Customs. These, together, comprised the Revenue for Government expenditure. During most of the Eighteenth century this expenditure was high. The country was almost permanently at war and the costs of the expanding Empire were, at that stage, far in excess of any return. In 1776, for example, the American colonies declared independence and within a few years Britain was also at war with France, Holland, Spain and a group of countries, known as the League of Armed Neutrality, led by Russia. This war finished in 1783 but within six years the French

Revolution had taken place and by 1793 war had again broken out. One reason for the American Revolution had been objection to paying taxes to Britain without Parliamentary representation (although technically they were included in the constituency of Greenwich). This was in spite of the fact that levels of duty were often lower than on equivalent products in Britain. Being proud of her democratic status, and duties being set by Parliament not imposed by the monarch, they were seen in this country as a necessary evil, to be avoided if possible but not a reason for insurrection.

Once Customs or Excise duties had been avoided then anyone handling the goods was, in effect, guilty of smuggling. So many people were involved between avoidance and consumption that the term "smuggler" was normally used to refer only to those responsible for the actual importing. The idea that smuggling was socially tolerable spread into the highest realms of society. Smugglers were sometimes known as "free traders". It was seen as enterprising, almost a victimless crime whereas, to the smugglers themselves, it was often an economic necessity to relieve their otherwise grinding poverty.

Because of the potential profits the capital for the enterprise was often put up by local businessmen, the "venturers", in all other respects upright members of society. This sometimes extended to the purchase, or even building, of vessels for the specific purpose of smuggling. The actual work, with its attendant risks, was carried out by fishermen, farm labourers and others who were seen as more expendable. The penalties for smuggling included fines to three times the contraband duty value, transportation for life or, in some circumstances, capital punishment. For simply smuggling, though, very few were caught. Such were the vested interests that even when brought to trial, "not guilty" verdicts were the usual result.

It was, however, still illegal and a serious drain on revenue. The Boards of Customs and of Excise took active measures to prevent the trade. Because a great deal of purely domestic traffic went by sea, as well as everything from abroad, both Boards operated fleets of Cutters, fast well-armed boats intended to patrol the coasts. They were often nearly identical to their adversary's ships, although some smuggling ships were bigger, better armed, faster and nearly always newer.

On land, each port had a Customs House where imports were declared and kept in bond. Ports included all their related creeks and inlets and the more important of these often had a Customs Office. The Port of Southampton included all landing places as far as just beyond Christchurch where the Port of Poole began. In those days the site of Bournemouth was empty, open heath. Landing places on the Isle of Wight came under the Port of Cowes, where the Collector of Customs for the whole district was based. Southampton and Poole were controlled as separate areas. Customers and Comptrollers were responsible, respectively, for Customs and Excise.

The actual work at the ports was carried out by Landwaiters (Customs) or Coastwaiters (Excise). Ships arriving were boarded by a Tide Surveyor and

THE CUTTER AND THE LUGGER
by kind permission of the National Maritime Museum

his deputy, a Tidesman, who stayed aboard until the cargo had been cleared.

To ensure, as far as possible, against illegal landing, the coast was divided into patrol areas under the charge of a Supervisor who commanded up to half a dozen Riding Officers. Very often the Riding Officers also had other occupations or were retired military or naval officers.

Whilst this may seem an impenetrable barrier to smuggling, it must be remembered that, in total, the Revenue Services employed relatively few men for a vast length of thinly inhabited coastline and only about forty cutters for the whole country. They were heavily outnumbered by the smugglers and outweighed by problems of sheer geography.

The difficulties were summed up by William Pitt in 1782, before he became Prime Minister, in a report to the Home Secretary: "... the strength and the number of men employed in that business is very formidable insomuch that in some districts they are capable of assembling from five hundred to a thousand men ... to receive the goods on the sea coast ... or less according to the quantity and ... probability of resistance; but in general greatly beyond anything that can be brought to oppose them."

Military units were often stationed near the coast in wartime to oppose potential invasion. In theory they could be called upon to assist against landings by smugglers. In order to get them to the right place at the right time some advance warning was necessary. This could be a two–way process, ensuring that the run took place somewhere else. The "Hovering Act" was intended to prevent vessels loitering within three miles of the coast, thus providing a sufficiently long approach to give the Revenue cutters a chance to catch them.

The real effectiveness of all these measures was well understood by the senior line officers of the Revenue services. William Arnold, the Collector of Cowes, had responsibility for the collection of duty between Southampton and Poole and the whole of the Isle of Wight. In October 1783, he reported to the Board of Customs on the difficulties he was facing. There had been an alarming increase in the level of smuggling during the previous three years, carried on by vessels too heavily armed for his cutters to stop. Much of the activity took place in daylight under observation of the Service who were impotent to prevent it. Large smuggling vessels often sailed in convoy with smaller ones to protect them and the stage had been reached where there was even an agreed scale of delivery charges depending upon the landing place and its potential dangers. Large rowing boats were used to offload smuggling ships at sea, thus making them "legal" when stopped. Many of these boats pulled so many oars that they could outpace the Revenue cruisers. Most of the known smuggling vessels which he listed were in excess of two hundred tons (the Revenue cutters were mostly in the fifty to one hundred and fifty ton bracket) and fast enough to make a landfall from outside the "hovering zone" without concern for the opposition beating them.

There were solutions, though, and with the hand of experience Arnold outlined them. Trebling the "hovering" limit would provide opportunities for more seizures, especially if naval ships were available in support. He suggested that a frigate be stationed off Poole. The fundamental weapon was to keep the shore parties waiting. This would dramatically increase the smugglers costs, reduce their profitability and destroy the trade. Large parties of men had to be paid and both they and animals had to be fed and sheltered. Laws to reduce the number of oars a boat could carry and the length it could be built to, would reduce part of his problem. Prize payment for such boat seizures, by the foot length would increase the enthusiasm of the Revenue officers for making captures. What was not required was that which the Board had suggested—more administrators.

Arnold was highly respected by his superiors and at least some of his suggestions were acted upon. Sadly the result was often an escalation of the level of antagonism and violence between the smugglers and their opponents. Once warships were involved the balance of power altered, yet the penalties remained the same. The navy tended not to back off. This could lead to gunfire with its attendant results. In May 1784, for example, four sailors of the *Swan* Revenue cutter required surgical attention and in October the same year the cutter *Speedwell* needed over one hundred pounds worth of repairs to shot damage.

Vessels seized continued to be sold at auction, if not bought by the Service. Thus, through intermediaries, owners had their property returned, including their inventories and guns. One of the ships owned by John Streeter and commanded by William May was seized and condemned for sale in 1783. The *Phoenix* was back under its original ownership and command structure by the following year. She was one of the pair of luggers which carried out one of the most audacious and, in terms of quantity, largest smuggling runs of the century. It took place at Christchurch in mid-July 1784. All the best elements of smuggling tales surround it. Starting with a cross channel pursuit, a landing in the face of authority, the arrival of sufficient force of law too late, a gun fight leading to murder, a small-boat action at sunset, treachery and a manhunt, it ended with a trial which, itself, was historic. William May commanded the *Phoenix's* sister ship at the Battle of Mudeford; William Arnold oversaw all the events from his office at Cowes. The profits went largely to John Streeter. It possesses, as a story, one overwhelming advantage—it really happened.

—— 2 ——

Time and Place

At the opening of the 1780's, Christchurch was a small town of around fifteen hundred inhabitants situated on a shingle bank at the confluence of the Stour and Avon rivers. These rivers flowed out to sea together through the harbour. Their beds formed the deep channel to the entrance, over a mile to seaward.

The town itself clustered around the ruined medieval castle and the Norman priory, closely bordered to the east by one of the Avon's two branches. To the south the land sloped down to the Quay with its mud berths and watermill. Here, every two weeks or so, one of the coasters which carried most of the town's trade would moor. Their cargoes were normally of wheat, because Christchurch had more milling capacity than the surrounding farms could employ. Sometimes they carried coal and other necessities. Outward bound went cargoes of flour and rushes. Most goods came by sea, because it was the least expensive means of transport and the roads were bad and often unsafe. This was at the end of the era before turnpike roads, canals and, a little later, railways, opened up the country to itself.

The High Street of Christchurch ran north west to the Bargate in the crumbling remains of a defensive wall built originally in Alfred's time. Beyond that was Bourne Heath, nothing but open land with a few cottages and fewer isolated hamlets, all the way to Poole, eleven miles distant. Beyond the Avon, eastwards, were the villages of Burton and Winkton and then the forest which stretched, effectively unbroken, to Southampton. Between the forest and the harbour a road ran through Stanpit to Mudeford, situated at the harbour mouth. Both places were straggling collections of roadside cottages. Mudeford was principally a fishing village with another mud berth at the Haven. Here there was an inn, the Haven House, with stables and outbuildings. These stood at the end of a sand spit. Across the Run—the harbour entrance—another sandbank led southwards to the rise of Warren Hill on what is now known as Hengistbury Head. In those days it was usually referred to as Christchurch Head. It covered a much larger area than it does today because the mining, which caused the massive erosion to take place, had yet to happen. On top of Warren Hill stood a summer-house, which made a first-class look-out.

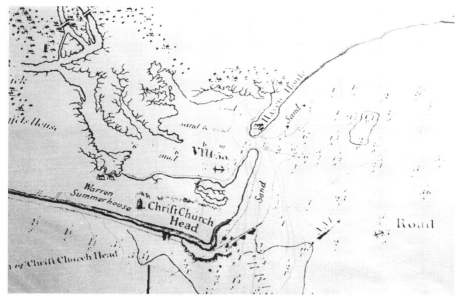

Lt. MURDOCH McKENZIE'S HYDROGRAPHIC SURVEY, 1785

Not being on a main road to anywhere, Christchurch was quite isolated. It developed according to its own needs, not to any grand plan. It was small, largely self-sufficient and peaceful.

Amongst the greatest differences between the Eighteenth century and the present was the lack of noise and artificial light. There was no background hum of traffic and railways and aircraft. The transport needs of the much smaller population were met by horse-drawn vehicles and ships which were driven by the breeze. What sounds there were were natural, unnatural ones stood out clearly. A musket shot, for example, could be heard miles away. At night there was a darkness unrelieved by the glow of street lights or head-lamps. In town open flame torches were used to illuminate building entrances, except for a few which had oil lamps. Candles or rushlights lit interiors. It was a different world where even the basic geography was not as it is today.

The isolation of Christchurch and its proximity to heath and forest made it an ideal landfall for smugglers. Its protected harbour and the look-out from the Head enhanced this further. The nearest military station was at Lymington, four hours march away. A day would be required to raise them as there were no telephones then. To guard this section of coast, the Revenue service maintained an office at number 10 Bridge Street. The building is still there. In charge, with overall responsibility, was a Supervisor, Joshua Stevens Jeans. His staff included Riding Officers Newsam, Reeks, Bursey and Noyce. All were local men, except Noyce, who was from Southampton. Jeans had been mayor of Christchurch four times.

NUMBER 10 BRIDGE STREET, CHRISTCHURCH
J. Jeans occupied offices in this building which made it, in effect, the Customs House

The Supervisor was paid about £50 a year, his officers rather less. This was not a particularly high salary, even by Eighteenth century standards. The Board of Customs expected this to be increased by a percentage paid on the value of seizures. It was intended to make them more vigilant. To maintain awareness of the activities of its agents, the Board required a quarterly statement together with copies of the journals kept by all officers. Jeans had long before trained his willing accomplices in the art of fraudulant completion of these journals. The principal smugglers had come to a simple, and for years very effective, arrangement. In exchange for not molesting them, Jeans received a part of each consignment at least equal in value to its seizure percentage. At reasonable intervals entire waggon-loads would be "seized" and impounded at the Customs store at Poole. By these means the Board remained unaware of the true state of affairs, Jeans and his officers enjoyed life and honest, casual observers were none the wiser. The only one of his officers who posed a threat was Noyce, but his journal reports could be amended before transmission to the Board. Not even he knew the depth of the deceit.

The duties of the officers included the inspection of all legitimate cargoes arriving at Christchurch. Most of these were discharged at the Haven Quay at Mudeford, saving ships the mile and a half of twisting channel up to the town. The public house on the quay provided a venue for any necessary, discreet meetings. The Haven House, having been converted to a drinking house about ten years before, was owned by Hannah Sellers. Its relative isolation, from the landward point of view, made it an ideal place for the smugglers to meet and plan, to lay over crews and victual waiting landing parties. Hannah's husband, John, had died in 1779 and she had taken over all his businesses, including those involving the storage and dispersal of contraband. Amongst the regular clientele of the house was John Streeter. In his mid-thirties, Streeter had lived in Christchurch since his marriage to Rose Button in 1773. He had a legitimate interest in maritime trade as, amongst other businesses, he operated coastal shipping services, mostly grain cargoes. He also ran, legitimately, a factory for manufacturing snuff. In June 1784 however, a consignment of his raw material—tobacco—had become of interest to the Board of Customs as its certificate was out-of-date. He had endeavoured to obtain it by having his brother-in-law named as the consignee. It was not intended to become a seizure but somewhere, something went amiss and the deception got out of hand. Only by quoting the regulation that prosecution would have to be at the Riding Officer's expense did Jeans avoid the danger of a court appearance for Streeter. Of the officers, Noyce was the one responsible for carrying the affair so far.

Streeter was known to be a smuggler. As long before as 1779 his ship *Phoenix* (the first of that name) had been seized with contraband. At first he had vehemently denied any knowledge of the affair, although he could not deny ownership. After various attempts at regaining his property, including threats and offers to pay a percentage of the duty, he eventually gave in and confessed, paying the full fine. In spite of all this he was considered a respectable family man, three of his six children being born by 1784.

William Parrott was also in regular attendance at the Haven House. The captain of the new *Phoenix*, he had something of a way with women, in Christchurch and Hamble at least. More or less everywhere that the *Phoenix* moored, Parrot had a mistress. No one but he knew if they thought of themselves as wives. Officially his ship was a coaster, trading in grain and general cargoes between the Isle of Portland and Chichester. In reality, many of these voyages, especially home-bound, touched the coast of France or the Channel Islands. It was quite common, in days of peace, to tack the whole way across when heading up wind down the Channel. As well as making for easier sailing and navigation, it provided a good reason for returning from an odd direction. Parrott was a flamboyant and quick-tempered character with a keen sense of self-preservation. Parrott's father often sailed with William May.

When both their vessels were alongside the two captains would drink together at the Haven House, providing useful mutual sources of information on the disposition of the Revenue cutters, potential cargoes and shipping news. May had been in Streeter's service for a number of years and normally commanded his latest ship, provided it was of a tonnage to suit his dignity. George Coombes, who had the same approach to women and responsibility as Parrott, occasionally sailed with May as mate. Around this time he was trying to conduct a romance with Widow Sellers.

Due to the limited numbers available from which to draw crews, both ships sailed with several members of the same families. There was a considerable leavening of men who were not local. Both captains were Londoners.

Most people in Christchurch in the year 1784 lived with smuggling as part, in some way, of their lives. Those who sat by the Haven House between voyages, watching the sails of distant warships pass the Needles towards Portsmouth, or who huddled over charts by rushlights, were most obviously involved. Many others helped occasionally with landing and distribution and most enjoyed the benefits of the increased volume of cash in the town. Most were no more violent or villainous than was normal. Apart from those directly involved, smuggling was thought no more sinful than the minor tax evasions of today. They lived their lives peacefully, married and brought up children. Some took an active part in community affairs, ran their businesses and obeyed, by and large, the laws of the country of which they were proud. The truly violent days of smuggling, when Revenue men were murdered for what they heard or saw, were two generations in the past.

All this was soon to change. Earlier in the year Streeter had taken delivery of a new lugger. She was nearly eighty feet in length and over seventy tons burden. He named her *Civil Usage* and put William May in command. Very late on July 1st she sailed from Christchurch on her first voyage in the trade.

The Battle of Mudeford

Early in the afternoon of July 5th, the lookout on the *Rose*, Revenue cutter sighted a sail. Although based at Southampton, the chosen duty of the *Rose* was to patrol the maze of rocks and islets between the major Channel Islands. Her purpose there was to discourage the running of contraband from France to the Islands where it could be secretly stored and transhipped, later, to the mainland. With the coast of the Cotentin peninsula only a matter of two or three hour's sailing, this was a near impossible task. She was a day out from Jersey, standing north towards a point between the Casquettes and Alderney. Her objective was to investigate the vessels that she ran across, ascertain their cargoes, check their papers and then escort them to a customs port. There were few opportunities for seizures at sea as no crime was committed by smugglers until the duty was avoided. They had to be caught in the act, if possible. This was a weakness in the system which was clearly recognised by those in the service. A complex pattern of bond certificates and dockets followed freight around and sometimes justified contraband. Yet it was her duty and so, as the sails of that disant, north-bound sighting shone against the north-eastern horizon, the *Rose* came round and gave chase.

The *Civil Usage*, Capt. William May, was four days out of Christchurch. After a night spent off Hurst on the Hampshire coast, opposite the Isle of Wight, she had sailed with a north-westerly breeze for Guernsey. There she took on a part cargo of wine, spirits and tea before sailing for Alderney where these were topped-up. She was now almost dead before the wind as she headed back towards Christchurch and was seen from the *Rose*.

Civil Usage was a lugger carrying her sails on two masts. Her crew comprised over thirty men and she was armed with twenty carriage and swivel guns, having been registered as a privateer whilst building. The war being over, she should have been reduced in armament, but such rules required checking.

Thus the chase began. Whilst both ships were fast, the *Rose* had the advantage of a greater angle to the breeze and, as the hours passed, gradually narrowed the gap. Although they had, so far, committed no crime, the concern aboard the lugger was that the Revenue cutter would escort her to a place where the payment of duty would be unavoidable if they were unlucky enough to be caught. As the two ships came level, still miles apart on their converging courses, the *Civil Usage* went about, heading just west of

'CHACE OF A CUTTER'
by kind permission of the National Maritime Museum

south and putting the breeze, as the cutter turned to follow, almost on her adversary's bow. Making good use of this advantage, the *Civil Usage* made for Alderney. The bulk of the island shielded her silhouette as the sun disappeared. Anchoring in the roadstead as darkness fell, she became invisible. Towards midnight she weighed and made sail for Cherbourg, where even the Revenue cutter couldn't follow.

Annoyed by the apparently miraculous escape of his quarry, but not at all surprised by her behaviour, the commander of the *Rose* spent the next two days scouring the roadsteads and harbours of the northerly Channel Islands, finding no sign of *Civil Usage*. After conferring with his officers he decided to patrol further north, between Alderney and Point de la Hague.

On the morning of July 9th the lugger worked her way out of Cherbourg and set sail again for Christchurch. The hills of the Cotentin peninsula were well down on the horizon when, to the west, a sail was sighted. Within an hour she could be clearly made out. The *Rose*, with the wind on her port quarter, was coming down fast whilst *Civil Usage* was close hauled and at a serious disadvantage. Very angry at his bad luck, Captain May ordered the lugger about and ran southwards again. *Rose* turned to follow but the distance was too great to overhaul her. By evening *Civil Usage* was once again safely in Cherbourg whilst the *Rose* cruised beyond the territorial limit, blockading and waiting.

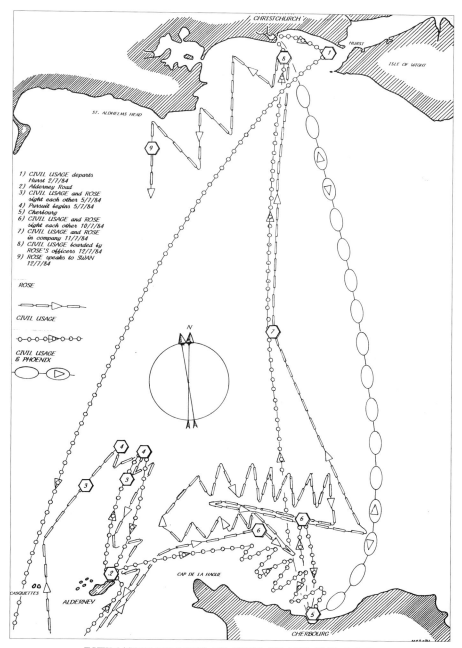

ESTIMATED TRACKS OF *CIVIL USAGE* AND *ROSE*
1/7/84 to 14/7/84

Captain May now had a serious problem. If he sailed with his cargo his chances of successfully running it ashore, with the *Rose* in close proximity, were poor. The same applied to escaping unseen. *Rose* might not always be in sight but her captain knew both their businesses. He could not fire on the *Rose*, for that would immediately be a capital offence, even if no one was hurt. Neither the Revenue service nor the Navy took kindly to those who moved from game to warfare.

By visiting his contacts in the port he arranged for his freight to be stored and discovered that there was sufficient already available to make up another cargo. Taking on fifty tons of gravel for ballast and with not a drop or ounce of contraband aboard, *Civil Usage* sailed for Christchurch, yet again, on the morning of the eleventh. The *Rose* came up with her halfway across.

In the days before wireless, the only methods of communication between ships were speaking trumpets at short range and flags at greater distances. Hailing was the usual means of attracting attention, a gunshot across the bow made a more forceful point. As *Civil Usage* approached Christchurch before dawn on the twelfth, the Revenue cutter hailed her, lowered a boat and despatched a boarding party. Frustrated as they were, the officers of the *Rose* could only return to their patrol as the lugger slipped into Christchurch completing an equally wasted voyage.

In the harbour was another of Streeter's fleet, the lugger *Phoenix* commanded by William Parrott. At daylight a number of *Civil Usage's* crew, feeling, perhaps, that they had had better, or worse luck than they deserved, left for home. The owner and his two captains, meanwhile, seated themselves in the Haven House to discuss the best ways of gaining the cargoes at Cherbourg and running them as soon as possible. The day was cloudy with glimpses of the sun. The breeze had veered from south-south-west in the morning to west by midday. The *Rose* was beyond the horizon bound for the Islands and no other sail was in sight. Pulling together crews for both vessels, they sailed in the late afternoon, reaching Cherbourg after an uneventful passage on the morning of the thirteenth.

Streeter, meanwhile, was busy in Christchurch collecting together the men, wagons and horses necessary to make up the receiving party. Once landed, the contraband had to be distributed to its various hiding places as rapidly as possible. It was necessary to have a different cart and crew for each destination, to off-load as quickly as they could and disappear. Timing was vital. Such a large group of men and gear would attract attention leading to obvious conclusions. More practically, if kept together too long, they would require food, shelter and additional payment. Provided the run was carried out quickly, sympathetic Revenue officers could justifiably turn a blind eye, arriving too late to prevent the incident. Those actually intent on stopping it would be at a serious disadvantage.

During the course of that afternoon and the following day, Streeter arranged for the assembly of upwards of three hundred men, a hundred wagons and four hundred horses. The amassing of such a force could not go unnoticed by the authorities and rumours reached the attention of Riding Officer James Noyce during the fourteenth. Noyce believed in his duty and went down to Mudeford, or near enough, to see what was going on. He rode back to town, passing stragglers bound for the beach on the way, and reported to his Supervisor, asking for instructions. Jeans had hoped that, of all his staff, Noyce would remain unaware of the proceedings. He had tried to ensure that his less reliable men were away from the area but had made a mistake with Noyce. His only recourse now was to tell his over-zealous subordinate to get elsewhere or go home, explaining that the two of them could not possibly prevent the landing and any attempt to do so could prove dangerous.

Less than satisfied with this response, Noyce left the office and taking backroads and byways until he was clear of the area, made for the Customs office and military station at Lymington.

The Customs cutter *Swan*, Captain George Sarmon, was based at Cowes. She patrolled between Beachy Head and Lyme Bay, often many miles out to sea. Stationed at the same port was the *Resolution*, a cutter in the Excise service, roughly the same size as *Swan* and with the same area of patrol, but much less heavily armed. Her commander, James Sarmon, was George's brother. Both cutters were at sea on July 12th. The *Swan*, cruising to the south-west of St. Alban's Head, sighted and spoke to another cutter, outward bound, early that morning. This was the *Rose* and from her George Sarmon learned of the abortive efforts of the *Civil Usage* over the past few days. He knew of May and Streeter and that they would probably try again.

Sarmon was experiencing a run of embarrassingly bad luck. In November of the previous year he had been in command of *Swan's* predecessor when she was wrecked at Hurst in a sudden squall. Personally contracted to William Arnold, it had been her maiden voyage. Only a few days ago, he had sent a party from his new cutter to board a known smuggling vessel, only to have them sent back stripped of all their weapons as the intended seizure sailed away. He desparately wanted to regain his earlier success. He also wanted revenge.

With a fresh breeze from the south-west he headed inshore for Poole Bay, commencing to patrol between there and Hurst. Although their sails were visible in the distance, he was just too late to observe the departure of the *Phoenix* and the *Civil Usage*.

The Customs service had taken William Arnold's advice of the previous year seriously. Now that the war was over the Royal Navy could spare ships to support the Revenue service. They could not provide a frigate for permanent patrol but they did the next best thing. In the early part of 1783 the sloop-of-war *Orestes*, Captain Hope-Bowers, was placed at the disposal of the Custom's service and stationed at Cowes. *Orestes* was quite a new ship. She had been built by the Dutch as a privateer, one of a pair, only two years previously. As the *Mars* she and her sister had been captured by the sloop *Artois*, Captain Macbride, and purchased by the Navy. Her shallow draught and brig-rig made her ideal for inshore work, whilst still capable of long, deep-sea passages. *Orestes* was nearly a hundred feet long on the gun-deck, carrying eighteen nine-pounder long guns and ten swivels. Her company numbered ninety-four, including six officers and sixteen marines.

In September 1783, Capt. Hope-Bowers relinquished his command due to ill-health and Francis Ross, First Lieutenant, who had been with the ship since she was purchased, acted until a replacement was posted. This was Commander James Ellis who took up his command on October 12th 1783.

Ellis was a very experienced officer. Commissioned on January 10th 1771 as Fourth Lieutenant in H.M.S. *Marlborough* (74 guns), he became First in the sloop *Fly* in 1777 and the following year was promoted to First in the frigate *Arethusa* (32 guns), Capt. Marshall. On July 17th 1778 *Arethusa*, part of Admiral Keppel's squadron, engaged the French frigate *Belle Poule* (36), Lt. Louis Chadeau de la Clocheterie, which fought her off, anchored amongst rocks to beat off two British ships-of-the-line and finally escaped back into harbour. Her seriously wounded commander was promoted Captain. In this action Ellis was also severely wounded. In October he was promoted Commander and spent the next two years in command of the armed ship *Princess of Wales* (20) in the North Sea. In 1780 he assumed command of the *Scout* (14), sloop-of-war, and in 1781 captured the French privateer *Le Glorieux* (12) whilst on convoy duty in the Irish Sea.

Within weeks of taking over *Orestes* he had made seizures, the kind of vessels the Revenue cutters would have been hard pressed to take on. In doing so his ship had suffered casualties. In May 1784 a large cutter, intent on making her run, had tried to run down one of *Orestes'* boats whilst they boarded another suspect. *Orestes'* people took the risks willingly, for every capture meant extra payment. Ellis did his best to gain as many as possible.

Unlike many naval officers, Ellis did not automatically reject people simply because they were in the Revenue service. He respected William Arnold who, in turn, considered Ellis a friend as well as a valued ally. Of the Revenue's sea officers, he had a rather less sanguine professional opinion. With his experience of action, small ships and coastal work Ellis was almost the ideal commander for *Orestes* on her present station.

In addition to Ellis and Ross, the officers of *Orestes* comprised two midshipmen, young boys learning the service, a surgeon and a sailing master, William Allen. Apart from his warrant as Master, Allen held a Commission from the Customs service. This was necessary for making seizures and arrests as only a limited number of people possessed such powers in law. Amongst the rest of the crew were twenty lesser warrant officers and specialists together with fourteen servants. The remainder were Able Bodied seamen, all volunteers as was necessary on such a station close to home.

At four in the morning of July 12th *Orestes* was off Christchurch bound for Weymouth. She narrowly missed the *Civil Usage* and *Rose* in the pre-dawn darkness. Leaving Weymouth at noon of the following day, she was again off Christchurch in the early hours of the fourteenth. She was anchored

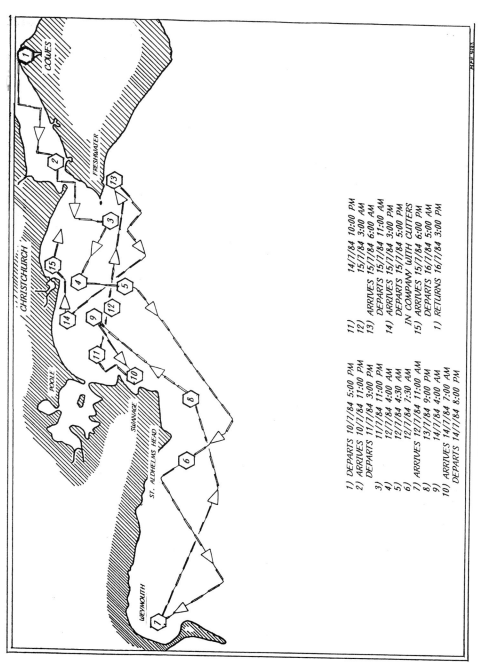

RECORDED POSITIONS H.M.S. ORESTES
10/7/84 to 16/7/84

1) DEPARTS 10/7/84 5:00 PM
2) ARRIVES 10/7/84 11:00 PM
   DEPARTS 11/7/84 3:00 PM
3) 11/7/84 11:00 PM
4) 12/7/84 4:00 AM
5) 12/7/84 4:30 AM
6) 12/7/84 7:30 AM
7) ARRIVES 12/7/84 11:00 AM
8) 13/7/84 9:00 PM
9) 14/7/84 4:00 AM
10) ARRIVES 14/7/84 7:00 AM
    DEPARTS 14/7/84 8:00 PM

11) 14/7/84 10:00 PM
12) 15/7/84 3:00 AM
13) ARRIVES 15/7/84 6:00 AM
    DEPARTS 15/7/84 11:00 AM
14) ARRIVES 15/7/84 3:00 PM
    DEPARTS 15/7/84 5:00 PM
    IN COMPANY WITH CUTTERS
15) ARRIVES 15/7/84 6:00 PM
    DEPARTS 16/7/84 5:00 AM
1) RETURNS 16/7/84 3:00 PM

in Swanage Bay between seven that morning and eight in the evening when she sailed for Freshwater on the south coast of the Isle of Wight.

Whilst *Swan* and *Orestes* pursued their patrols throughout Wednesday July 13th, the *Civil Usage* and *Phoenix* sailed from Cherbourg. Each vessel carried four tons of tea and a total of forty-two thousand gallons of spirits. In Christchurch Streeter arranged his reception party whilst at the Custom's office Joshua Jeans deployed his men. The Riding Officers had long since learned to falsify their records and obtain just enough seizures, as well as contraband for themselves, to avoid the suspicion of higher authority. The exception to this was Noyce. Jeans had already ordered him out of the way but he had acted too late, for Noyce already knew of the imminent run.

One of the problems involved in any affair which relied upon sailing ships was that of timing. The voyage from Cherbourg to Christchurch, a distance of about sixty nautical miles, could take anywhere between eight hours and three days. On this occasion, sailing a close reach to the light breeze from the west-north-west, the heavily laden luggers took about twenty-four hours. At around mid-day, the lookout on Christchurch Head sighted the sails far to the south and sent word to Streeter. The members of the landing party not already assembled on the beach, dispersed around the town and nearby hamlets were summoned. They included a number of the crew from *Civil Usage's* previous voyage. The beach just north of the harbour entrance became a scene of intense activity as wagons were prepared, men hurried to join the assembly and sentries were stationed to watch for the Revenue men, except, of course, Jeans and his associates.

The harbour entrance then was different from today. Although it was less tortuous there was still a bar to negotiate a few hundred yards off the mouth. This was partly due to the drift effect caused by the ruins of a three-hundred yard stone mole to the south, part of short-lived harbour improvements, then a century old. This meant that ships bound for the Haven had to pass the entrance northwards, go about and circumvent the end of the bar. As they did so the breadth of Avon beach faced them, shelving to a good depth at high water but drying out some distance at low. Between there and the Haven House the land decreased in height, becoming a dune-covered sandspit. Various attempts had been made, over the years, to protect this from erosion by adding timber pilings. Beyond all this, to the west, the tower of the Priory was visible, a mile away across the marshes of the northern part of the harbour.

Due to the landform of the Isle of Wight and the channels either side, Christchurch enjoys two high waters per tide. After first high the tide ebbs slightly but then rises again, giving up to six hour's high water. *Civil Usage* and *Phoenix* needed high water to get reasonably close to the landing party. As James Noyce made his way to Lymington and the *Swan* lay off Yarmouth, the two luggers slowly stood in for the beach.

There now occured what, to Streeter, must have seemed the substance of his nightmares. Coming from the direction of Hurst and the Needles passage

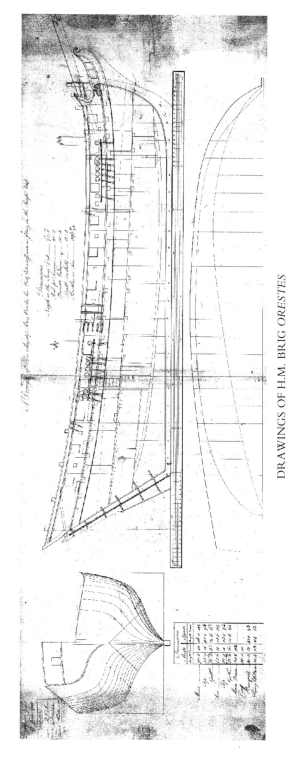

DRAWINGS OF H.M. BRIG ORESTES

made after her capture from the Dutch by kind permission of the National Maritime Museum

was another sail. It was the *Resolution* commanded by James Sarmon. Although still several hours away, her approach meant that the run would now be observed. As Streeter and his gang watched, the cutter spread her topsail and bore down towards them.

Civil Usage and *Phoenix* rounded the bar and beached in mid-afternoon. Activity now became frantic as they were unloaded of nearly five thousand casks of spirit and four hundred chests of tea. Men ran into the water and struggled out laden with a hundredweight tub or chest. A beachmaster directed the wagons for loading and as each was filled it was hauled away towards the heath or the forest. As the luggers were lightened they floated higher, making unloading that much more difficult. Some of the carts were driven into the water alongside and loaded directly. Midway through these proceedings John Bursey, one of the Riding Officers, arrived. No one stopped work as he approached Streeter. Glancing around at the luggers and the long lines of carts, and casting an eye towards the still distant cutter, he enquired whether the officers' casks were yet unloaded. Streeter pointed to a stack of over a hundred tubs a little way up the beach, each marked with the letter "F". A squad was ordered to load a line of carts kept separate from the majority. When this was done Bursey touched his hat in salute to Streeter and his captains, wheeled his horse and led his "seizures" from the beach.

As the unloading proceeded and wagons and carts were despatched the number of men available reduced. The loading of the last few carts was clearly seen from the deck of the Excise cutter but there was nothing to be done. Sarmon didn't need to count his adversary's gun ports to realise that he was in no position to prevent what he could see. His cutter carried only eight four-pounders. Opening fire on a force five times his in terms of guns, eight times in terms of weight of broadside and five or six times in terms of manpower, even at this late stage in the run, was a greater risk than he was prepared to take. He stood the cutter off beyond gunshot range and watched. He could at least bear witness to the events later. Nonetheless, he was furious because a large part of his income stemmed from the profits of seizures.

With the unloading completed, a party of men was organised by Captain May to drag the *Civil Usage* around into the harbour behind the Haven House. Most of her crew helped, except for a few with boathooks or on the tiller. A few minutes later Captain Parrott, having made similar arrangements, followed with the *Phoenix*. As they did so a boat from the cutter was rowed up and a demand made to board and inspect. The men hauling the *Civil Usage*, by now clearly round the point, couldn't hear the reply but the boat pulled away and a few minutes later the cutter made sail and stood away to the south.

With the luggers now secure in their berths, the crews dispersed back into town, except for those who chose the hospitality of the Haven House. Twelve miles to the east, the troops at Lymington were being issued their orders. As darkness came on they began to patrol the paths and trackways of the forest hoping to come across at least some of the goods as they were taken into hiding.

Knowing full well that, having been seen running contraband, his ships would be forfeit and knowing, too, that help for the Excise cutter was probably close at hand, Streeter and his captains began preparing their ships for sea. He had already re-purchased the *Phoenix* once from the Customs service and the cost, together with intermediaries commissions, ate deeply into his profits. He must avoid their seizure at all costs. Whilst they could do much of the necessary work themselves overnight, with the help of the few remaining men, they could only make a start on ballasting.

Sarmon needed assistance. In order to gain it he needed to send physically to search. There was no other way, as evening fell on July 14th, of communicating. The sun had now set, the sky beyond Purbeck turning blue from pink, black towards the Isle of Wight with the sea the colour of ink. The *Swan* was at Yarmouth and somewhere to the south was *Orestes*. Sarmon was determined not to lose the whole catch, regardless of who he had to share it with. The crew of the *Resolution* was not sufficient to provide prize crews, even if they could capture the luggers on their own. The same problem precluded using both of the cutter's boats to search out their compatriots. As the evening deepened a light was seen away to the south-west, moving slowly eastwards. Sarmon guessed, or at least hoped, that it was *Orestes* and despatched his boat, already in the water and rigged, to intercept her. In the event he was right.

Just after dawn on the following morning William May rode to the house of William Burden, a fisherman, in Christchurch. This house was often used by members of his crews laying-over and he found several of them there. Together, they returned to Mudeford where they continued to ballast the luggers. Their urgency was heightened by a report of another cutter in the bay. This was the *Swan*, unaware of the previous day's activities, patrolling towards Poole. By now the cargo was safely away, apart from Bursey's toll, now redistributed by Jeans. None had fallen into the hands of the various authorities hunting for it.

Out in Poole Bay *Swan* had been seen from *Resolution* and the two met off Poole bar a little after mid-day. Earlier, at around ten, the cutter's boat was sighted from *Orestes* as the sloop lay off Freshwater. Like those aboard *Swan* her people had no idea of the previous day's events. Now summoned to aid the Excise service *Orestes* weighed, cleared the Needles and came up with the two cutters at three in the afternoon.

Back behind Christchurch Head the ballasting of the two luggers was nearly completed. Burden and other members of the crew continued the backbreaking labour of shifting baskets of gravel into the holds of *Civil Usage* and *Phoenix*. Each required nearly fifty tons. In the Haven House Parrott and May heard reports of the sloop's arrival and realised that escape, now, would be a close call.

Having finished the ballasting, Burden, William Webb, Henry Voss, George Bond, Joseph Seven and Bone Tucker, all of the *Civil Usage*, came ashore and, understandably, made for the Haven House for refreshment. With other members of the crew recently arrived May and Parrott began their final preparations for sea.

Hove-to in the bay and drifting in the light and variable breezes which fluttered between periods of calm, the three King's vessels lay. Aboard *Orestes*, with Ellis in the chair, a conference was held to decide upon a course of action. As this progressed the squadron drifted slowly eastwards with the tide. The outcome was simple. The three would closely blockade the harbour mouth, send in their boats with armed seamen and marines and cut out the luggers. There was some debate over the division of the spoils but Ellis cut this short. Such matters could wait until there was something to argue about. At around five the flotilla made sail towards the Head. William Allen required all his skill, trimming and re-trimming the sails, to get any ground covered at all in the fluky and unreliable airs of the afternoon. His duty, later, would be to make the actual seizures and any arrests. As Christchurch Head loomed closer Ellis ordered *Orestes* cleared for action. His experience had shown him the result of shot splinters, so the boats were lowered, filled with the more portable and fragile fittings and towed astern. The guns were loaded and run out. Just before six *Orestes*, *Swan*, *Resolution* and *Orestes* longboat, which had been carrying messages between the three, rounded the Head and drew steadily towards the harbour entrance. *Civil Usage* and *Phoenix* were now trapped.

As the squadron anchored off the bar John Streeter came up from Christchurch to the Haven House at the gallop. He and his captains may well have risked intimidating *Resolution*, possibly even the *Swan* but *Orestes* dramatically altered the odds. At nearly four hundred tons she far outweighed her opposition. From her anchorage the nine guns of her broadside covered the only possible exit. Together they could hurl nearly three-quarters of a hundredweight of iron shot, reasonably accurately, over half a mile. The range to the harbour entrance was about half that. This ship was built for war and Streeter, May and Parrott knew something of her officers' quality. Knowing that their vessels were lost, the smugglers' thoughts now turned to reducing the damage. Streeter ordered all his men to remove as much gear as they could from *Civil Usage* and *Phoenix* in the time remaining. This included masts, spars, guns and sails as well as the ships' boats, which were sunk alongside later in the evening. Burden and his mates tumbled back to the luggers and began removing the sails which they stored in the outhouses of the inn.

Amongst the squadron the next stage of the action was being prepared. *Orestes'* boats were already in the water and these were now joined by those from the *Resolution* and the *Swan*, making half-a-dozen in all. Into each went the pre-arranged crews, *Orestes'* boats with six marines in each, sitting to attention in the sterns, their muskets upright. The second boat was *Orestes'*

HAVEN HOUSE MUDEFORD
The nearer end of this building was the Haven Inn in 1784. It is now called the Dutch House

pinnace, commanded by William Allen, who, because of his Customs Board commission, assumed overall command of the expedition. The marines were all under the command of Sergeant Jacob Carey who was in the leading boat.

On shore the efforts to clear the luggers of their gear re-doubled. Captains May and Parrott began handing out muskets and ammunition to the trusted members of their regular crews. These included Jonathan Edwards, Henry Voss, George Coombes, David Harris and David Bell, all of whom had sailed with the contraband.

The tide was now beginning to ebb and the boats' approach was slow and through uncharted waters. The pinnace, at 26 feet in length, had a greater draft than the others and as she approached she ran onto a sandbank. William Allen, in the bow, stepped out to lighten her and push her off. As he did so several of the armed smugglers, who had taken up positions behind the luggers and the sand-filled pilings, opened fire. Allen, in the act of climbing back into the pinnace, was struck in the thigh. It was not a serious wound but it knocked him over. As he recovered himself and moved forward he was hit again, this time in the body and much more seriously. Ordering the boats on he collapsed, one of the seamen did what he could to stem the bleeding and make the Master comfortable on the bottom boards, below the level of the gunwhale. The leading boats were now around the point, their marines returning fire as they ran alongside the luggers.

It is no easy act to board a seventy ton ship from a small boat in the face of heavy fire. Using the bulwarks as a shield, the smugglers fired down into the boats whilst the Revenue tenders stood off and tried to give covering fire over the heads of the nearer crews. In *Orestes* Corporal Archibald Carmichael and his few remaining marines kept up fire at the breastworks, assisted by the ship's crew. Ellis, with no detailed information about what was happening, could only watch the increasing pall of gunsmoke through which flickered the occasional flash of fire or shadow of movement. In the longboat one of the marines fell, his arm shattered and one of the pinnace's crew took a ball in the shoulder, throwing him backwards off the thwart. Midshipman Hyatt was screaming at the men to board the luggers and carry them by storm whilst in the other boat Sergeant Carey was considering the option of tactical retreat. Two facts were obvious to him. Firstly he could not board the luggers without risking heavy losses and, secondly, they could not go anywhere in any case. Under covering fire from his marines, Carey and Hyatt hastily conferred. In the bow William Allen was still conscious and his safety now became a matter of concern. At that moment the firing from the luggers ceased. As quickly as possible the marines boarded, to be met with renewed fire from the windows of the Haven House and the nearby outhouses. The luggers were deserted but were also solidly aground.

Whilst this was going on, Burden and several other occasional members of the smuggling crew took shelter in the bedrooms of the Haven House. When the firing slackened they escaped downstairs and out and gaining the sandspit, began to make their way towards the town. The reason for the reduction in firing was that the smugglers' ammunition was running low. William May took Streeter's horse and galloped for Christchurch, passing Burden and his friends on the way. He wheeled on them, blasted them as cowards and then, shaking with anger, raced on. Not long afterwards they saw him riding back carrying a cask of ammunition. A short while later they heard the renewed firing.

The sun was now setting. Carey and Hyatt concluded that they could not cut out the craft at that state of the tide and were concerned to get Allen back to *Orestes* and the surgeon. Accordingly they withdrew to the boats and began the passage back to the squadron. Still under occasional fire, the marines shot at anything on the shore which moved.

The semi-conscious Master and the other wounded were brought aboard *Orestes* as the sun set. William Allen was carried to his cabin, the others to the lower deck, forward, where the warrant officers' mess was situated, their sea-chests becoming operating tables. Soon afterwards the surgeon reported to Commander Ellis. The marine's arm might mend, the other wounded would recover. William Allen's wound was mortal. Too much damage had been done for the surgeon's techniques and skill to repair. It was only a matter of time.

Against the afterglow Ellis could see the silhouette of people re-boarding the luggers. He ordered his main armament fired in succession followed by that of the cutters.

On board the luggers the crews ducked as far as they could as the low howl of the shot moaned overhead, sending fountains of water, sand and mud skywards immediately beyond them. A few musket shots were returned until the squadron fired again, damaging the buildings and breastworks along the shore. It was now too dark for accurate shooting and the firing ceased.

Half an hour or so later the smugglers began to return to Christchurch and disperse themselves around the town. Burden watched them. The last to arrive were Captains May and Parrott. At three the next morning it was quite calm. The tide was now rising again. Using the boats, Ellis ordered the two cutters towed inshore and anchored in the channel. Springs, additional lines, were fitted to their anchor cables to enable their broadsides to be swung in the direction of any fire. Under the command of Francis Ross the boats entered the harbour once more, went alongside the luggers and grappled them. There was no opposition to their boarding, everyone had gone. The luggers were towed from the harbour.

Fitful and variable breezes stirred the otherwise still surface of the bay. As the sun rose over the distant, misty silhouette of Hurst Point it reflected a path of blood towards the squadron. *Orestes* had suffered casualties, no-one knew the losses ashore. None of her people was happy at having to fight their own countrymen, in spite of the value of the seizure. At five, led by *Orestes* and with their prizes in tow of the cutters, the little fleet weighed and stood eastwards. There was no-one on the beach to watch them depart.

At six, in his tiny, coffin-like cabin on the lower deck, attended by Surgeon Taylor and Alexander Proctor, his assistant, William Allen died.

—— 4 ——

"... For the Better Discovering and Bringing to Justice ..."

The arrival of *Orestes* at Cowes signalled the opening of a barrage of newspaper articles seething with indignation at the murder of a King's warrant officer. The squadron's entire casualties had been amongst *Orestes'* people. The prizes, however, had been physically towed by the cutters commanded by the Sarmon brothers. There was some disagreement as to how the benefits of the seizure should be divided, compounded by the fact that each vessel in the squadron belonged to a different service.

With his report to his Flag Officer, Ellis included a memorial for transmission to the Treasury requesting that his ship's company receive the full allocation. This view was entirely endorsed by the newspapers locally.

Reports were a fundamental part of life in the Navy and Revenue services. Everything was noted and accounted for, especially where any expenditure was involved. From before the ships anchored in the roadstead, at around three on Friday afternoon, this work was in progress. The Sarmons prepared their documents for William Arnold, Commander Ellis for the Flag Officer, Portsmouth, the Admiralty, the Treasurer and the Collector of Customs. Francis Ross wrote in his support. The surgeon carried out his post mortem on William Allen, preparing for the inquest.

This was held the following day in the Town Hall at Cowes. The only witnesses were, not unnaturally, from the side of the authorities. All the principal witnesses had attended these things before, which made them no less unpleasant. James Sarmon explained how he had come upon the luggers as they approached the harbour but, being unable to stop them, had sent for assistance and been forced into the position of a helpless observer. James Ellis briefly outlined events from the arrival of his ship to her departure. Thomas Taylor described how Allen, struck by the first ball, had immediately received his second, ultimately fatal wound. The shot, entering from the right, had penetrated his liver and stomach. He had lingered for twelve hours and died on passage.

The newspaper correspondents, and that is exactly what they were in those days, struggled furiously to keep up with their notes in an atmosphere of increasing indignation. Amidst an avalanche of facts—times, positions, names—a few errors appeared in print. The atmosphere of anger, though, was clearly divided between the act of murder and the shame that the undoubted bravery which the smugglers possessed was not better directed.

Outside the stifling atmosphere of the courtroom a perfect summer's day developed. In the sparkling air of the roadstead cat's paws of ruffled water played between *Orestes* and the moored cutters. Whilst her officers gave evidence, the crew of the sloop cleared and cleaned their ship. Alongside the Custom's quay *Civil Usage* and *Phoenix* lay, bare hulls waiting for condemnation, powder burns on their gunwhales and splintered bullet holes testifying to their crews' efforts to save them.

In the courtroom a decision was reached. The death of William Allen had been wilful murder. The assailant was unknown but he had been aided and abetted by William May and William Parrott.

What the smugglers had hoped to achieve was the subject of much discussion both in the town and aboard the various ships. The idea of their attempting to escape was easily grasped, even that of trying to save as much of their gear as possible when that was denied them. The danger to themselves of firing on the landing party and on the *Orestes* herself would normally have outweighed all other considerations. It must have been obvious at the moment of the sloop's arrival that, in the end, the smugglers could not win. To risk the gallows to save the re-purchasing cost of a lugger, even a new one, seemed out of balance. The run had been made, the goods dispersed and the profit assured. Almost certainly the opening shot had been accidental. After that the affair had gained its own internal momentum. Once Allen was wounded events could take no other course. Ellis cared for his men, if not particularly for the Revenue service. His experience made his reaction inevitable. The philosophy was simple, if fired upon return the compliment harder and more effectively.

Not only Ellis' reaction was inevitable. With a verdict of murder recorded and names quoted the procedure now began which ended, eighteen months later, in the High Court of Admiralty and Execution Dock.

By the time the inquest finished those responsible for the murder and their comrades-in-arms, unaware of Allen's death let alone the verdict, had returned to their other lives. All, that is, except Streeter, May and Parrott. Streeter had to come to terms with the loss of his investment. In his view such things were business expenses. The run had been successful and the profits would roll in. New ships could be built or purchased, May and Parrott might yet obtain new commands. Throughout the weekend the troops from Lymington continued their patrols and searches but discovered nothing.

Throughout Sunday the weather gradually changed. As the crew of *Orestes* completed clearing and cleaning the gentle breeze backed to west-south-west and began to increase. By evening a fresh gale was blowing. The ships in Cowes road snubbed at their cables and leaned to the gusts. Early on Monday morning the weather deteriorated further. Heavy squalls now struck them in their anchorage and driving rain reduced visibility to yards.

At seven in the morning, as the ship rolled sharply at her moorings, Ellis ordered both watches aloft and had the top-gallant masts struck and lowered to the deck. With the centre of gravity adjusted *Orestes* rode more easily. On that day it was essential that she could be left with just an anchor watch.

The arrangements for William Allen's funeral were completed by midday and late in the afternoon *Orestes'* boats were launched to take the party ashore. Allen's coffin, his hanging-cot for the past commission, was lowered, flag-draped, into the pinnace. Guarded by a marine detachment and with Ellis and Ross in the stern as escort, the boat pulled across the turbulent water to the landing stage. Other officers and marines followed in the longboat whilst hired shore-boats brought the remainder of the crew, in Sunday attire despite the continuing rain.

Led by a party of marines, their arms reversed and at the slow march to the beat of the quarter-drum, the coffin was taken up through the steep, rain soaked streets. Silent crowds lined the way as the procession progressed to the churchyard of St. Mary's, the parish church of Cowes. The coffin was carried by Allen's mess-mates, the senior ratings and midshipmen. Ellis, Ross and the senior warrant officers brought up the rear. With due solemnity, sadness and military honours William Allen completed his voyage at the age of only twenty-five.

The day after the funeral, the gale still raging and no let up in the rain, life began to return to its usual routine. In the morning, whilst *Orestes* was revictualled with beer and beef from Portsmouth, William Arnold prepared his report to the Board of Customs, together with more local enquiries necessary to begin tracing the killers. He was aware that, in such an action fought so close to town, rumours would abound. The number of people involved was a benefit. It increased the opportunities for an unguarded word to reach his agents or even, perhaps, for someone to be persuaded to give deliberate information. All the arguments, clashes and vendettas within the group could be played upon. Somewhere many people knew what had happened. He only had to find one of them.

With the gale rattling the windows of the Sixteenth century Customs House across the river in East Cowes, in which he had his office, he surveyed the roadstead through the rain. The *Swan* rode there with *Orestes*, her masts made stubby by lack of top-gallants. *Resolution* had moved up river to Newport. Soon the weather would clear. The endless task of patrol would begin again. There would be more seizures and further resistance. Arnold believed, like Ellis, that the best course to follow, if opposed, was to stamp down hard. In the past he had suggested to the Board that the harsher penalties of an earlier age be re-introduced. The most effective action must immediately be taken to bring the criminals to book.

With this in mind he wrote first to the Supervisor at Christchurch, Joshua Jeans. Although he knew that not all officers with commissions from the Board of Customs possessed the highest standards of integrity, Arnold had no reason to suspect, at this stage, that Jeans was less than straightforward.

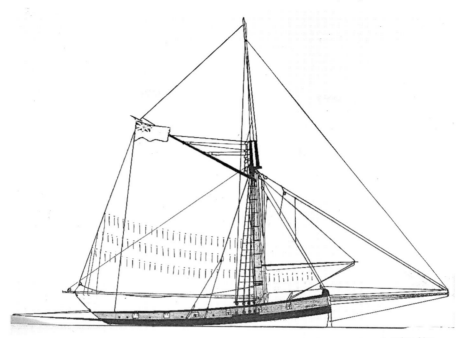

water line

REVENUE CUTTER *SWAN*
The appearance of H.M. Cutter Resolution would have been very similar

Whilst he had received no word of report from Christchurch and had no idea of the disposition of the Riding Officers there, any number of reasons could account for this. Reports could be easily delayed, there was, after all, a gale blowing. They could, even at that moment, be about to apprehend the smugglers. He told Jeans what had been heard at Cowes and requested his utmost efforts in gaining information to bring the murderers to justice. In doing this he unknowingly commenced the means by which most of the guilty escaped, for Jeans carried the warning to them and continued to be their source of up-to-date information on the activities of the authorities.

Arnold now prepared his report for the Board of Customs. In his usual manner he was precise and offered a course of action. In addition to forwarding crew lists found aboard the captured luggers, he suggested a financial reward and a pardon for anyone providing information leading to arrests. The Board heeded his recommendations. The lists, together with later information, formed the basis of the warrants for arrest for smuggling which appeared later in the year. On July 23rd. the Board agreed to advertise a reward and this was copied to the south coast Customs houses three days later. Two hundred pounds and a pardon was offered to anyone whose information led to the arrest of two or more of the smugglers involved. The only exclusion was that of the actual killer. It appeared in the local newspapers during the following week.

Whilst this document was being prepared the weather moderated, *Orestes* replaced her top-gallants, completed her repairs and returned to patrol on July 25th. On the day that the local papers published their accounts of William Allen's funeral she was well down the Solent, carrying on the task for which he had died. The weather remained unsettled, the wind backing and veering almost by the hour and varying from calm to gales and back in one watch. She ended the month storm bound in the entrance to Poole Harbour. That last day of July the weather moderated and at nine in the morning she prepared for sea, beating back to Cowes against a fresh north-easterly. A fortnight later she arrived at Portsmouth, having again completed a patrol. On the same day, by one of those occasional ironies, she was joined by another sloop, *Plyades* from Plymouth. *Plyades* was her sister ship built, sailed and captured together back in 1781.

By now Jeans had had adequate opportunity to ensure the dispersal of the smugglers, at least the leading ones. His concern was as much for himself as for them. Any of them could reveal how he had been operating for the past several years. Streeter, May and Parrott had escaped to the Channel Islands where they were fairly safe from arrest. Many of the minor characters could not do this. By the beginning of August the pressure on some of them was increasing. The rumour of a general pardon had been scotched, not only by the reward notice but by other news as well. The idea had begun along with another rumour of a change in the law and penalties. Because so many wanted to believe it, it became credible. It did not, though, make it fact.

So far no arrests had been made, neither had any response been had from Joshua Jeans. Suspicions were beginning to grow, certainly in Arnold's mind, and amongst the Board. On August 20th Arnold's recommendations were justified. William Burden, one of the crew of the *Civil Usage*, presented himself at the Customs office in Lymington. Before the Deputy-Collector and the town's peace officer he made a detailed statement of what he knew of the events of the previous month. Wherever possible he put names to actions explaining, in part, the motives and supporting the statements of the squadron's officers. He thought that Parrott had fired the first shot. May, William Harris and David Bell had also been seen firing. The two captains were the last to leave the scene. Whether he gave the evidence from genuine concern at the committing of a murder, fear, self-preservation or antago-nism, Burden left a richer man. The two hundred pounds reward which he later received was the equivalent of four year's pay for the captain of a cutter, fourteen year's for one of the seamen. Then there was the King's pardon. He was no longer guilty of any offence. Such things could not protect him from his late partners or, later, from the press-gang. William Burden quietly disappeared.

H.M. cutter *Expedition* belonged to the Royal Navy. Late in August she was despatched to the Channel Islands to gain information on, and hopefully arrest, those who had escaped there. With Lt. Crook, her commander, sailed another of the Sarmon family, Francis. As well as being a midshipman he also held a Customs commission to enable him to make arrests. At Guernsey they found the Danish brig *Ebeneezer* in quarantine having lost all of her crew to disease on the voyage from Zante. She was now manned with the rabble collected in her brief stops along the northern coast of France. Crook was concerned that the smugglers might trade with the ship, thus increasing the danger of infection. He reported this to Arnold who added it to his own suspicions. It was possible that the smugglers might use this ship to recommence their trade. He recommended that the ship be either guarded by someone in addition to the quarantine officers, or towed somewhere else.

During late August and early September, as summer gave way to autumn, a number of other people came forward to the authorities. They included both participants and witnesses. None of them presented themselves at Christchurch. The list of names of those wanted on suspicion steadily grew. In September, finally exasperated beyond endurance by the behaviour of his own Supervisor, James Noyce went before the Deputy-Collector at Lymington and signed an affidavit.

Issuing warrants for arrest was one thing, executing them was quite another. With Jeans aware of every move and each name, unknown to themselves the authorities were creating their own difficulties. These names, of course, were also known to others. May had already returned to the mainland, at Streeter's instigation, to check the potential for further runs. He searched out the one person he could absolutely trust, George Coombes. For some days they travelled the area secretly, at night, renewing contacts and preparing business. Then they were warned that the warrants had been issued and went into hiding at Hamble while they awaited an opportunity to escape back to the Channel Islands.

Near Hamble lived Thomas Morse. Morse's father had been a Riding Officer but had been dismissed for collusion with the smugglers in his district. His mother had gone mad. Young Morse had subsequently had to support them both, together with a number of other members of the family and associates. Through his father's old contacts he heard of the whereabouts of the fugitives and saw an opportunity for clearing the family name, at least in part. The means by which he gained this information turned out to be a two-edged sword. May and Coombes were hustled elsewhere before the militia arrived. May escaped to France, Coombes returned to his old haunts, temporarily remaining under Jean's protection.

Although the attempt at capture had been a failure, Morse petitioned the Board of Customs for a position at Southampton, even offering to pay a reduced salary to whoever was ousted for his gain. Of the two possibilities, the incumbents of the Southampton posts, Mr. Thring had lost the use of his hands whilst Mr. Cage suffered from palsy and was eighty years old. The Board sent the petition to their agents at Portsmouth and Southampton. No-one in either of those places had ever heard of him.

As autumn deepened and the weather became less reliable, the opportunities for further enterprises by Streeter and the others diminished. Fishermen put to sea less frequently. Those tied to the land prepared for ploughing. It is not easy, now, to appreciate the effect which the onset of winter had on society two hundred years ago. To most intents and purposes a great deal closed down for three or more months. Rain washed out roads making travel inland all but impossible. At sea, sudden storms made movement equally hazardous. At the beginning of October the Board of Customs applied, through their solicitor, for warrants to arrest for evasion of duty on twenty-seven individuals regarding two separate runs. Twenty-one were related to the Mudeford incident.

Warrants were still out for arrest on suspicion for a number of others not on the Board's list. Just before Christmas news reached Southampton that two of the wanted men had been seen in Guernsey. Despite the lateness of the season and the bitter and stormy weather an Excise cutter was despatched, with a supernumerary with powers of arrest, to collect them. She returned just before the year turned and moored at Cowes. The Collector now waited for the Board's further instructions. The two prisoners, Bone Tucker and Guernsey Jemmy, were confined aboard the cutter. On New Year's Day Guernsey Jemmy somehow escaped. Arnold was convinced that some officer of the Excise service had colluded in this, as to swim to shore at that time of year would have been fatal. A further warrant was issued for his arrest but no trace of him was found.

Tucker went before the magistrate on January 2nd. He had an alibi. As the squadron's boats had approached he had run off in such haste that he had left his personal gear behind. He had the good fortune to meet, as he left the scene at the height of the firing, someone who recognised him and spoke for him at the hearing. There was no evidence that he had fired any shots or assisted those who had in any way. He was released. Very soon afterwards luck ran out for George Coombes and two of his crew, Henry Voss and Jonathan Edwards. Edwards' name was not on the list of those wanted for smuggling. The statements of the various witnesses added up to a rather more serious accusation. They were arrested for murder.

They appeared at Winchester Assize on February 20th, before Sir Beaumont Hotham. No further arrests had been made during their confinement in Winchester gaol. It was fully expected that, as witnesses could be easily called, it being only about thirty miles to either Christchurch or Portsmouth and rather less to Southampton, that the trial would go ahead. This did not happen. The victim had been a King's warrant officer. He had been wounded and died below the high tide line. Hotham felt that his court was not competent to try the offence under those circumstances and so, after a rehearsal of the written evidence, the accused were put back in gaol. The case was passed to the High Court of Admiralty, which sat in the Old Bailey. On February 27th Coombes, Edwards and Voss were transferred to Newgate.

Whilst these events were developing, Arnold continued with the more mundane aspects of his work. Few of these now related to the outrage of the previous July. He had already sent details of the two luggers to be condemned to the Board and was by now dealing with other matters, the value of other seizures, ownership of boats and so on. Late in January, just after the arrests, the Board sent a directive to its south coast Collectors and Deputies to keep a good watch for the five remaining fugitives on the warrant for murder. It was to be passed to all their sea-going officers, local staff and the officers of any naval vessels whom they might meet in the course of their duties. In February the officer who had arrested Tucker and Jemmy found himself having to explain to the Board why he had claimed expenses for the crossing to the Channel Islands when he had travelled in one of the service's cutters.

Information now reached the Collector at Southampton of the whereabouts of William May. Experience had shown that this informant's news tended to be worth following up. Although some expense was put into searching, including paying the informer, May was not found.

Streeter, in the meantime, had discovered that he was only wanted for duty evasion, not murder. This was a more familiar hazard. He also knew that the warrant only applied for two court terms. After that the Board would re-appraise the cost-effectiveness of continuing the prosecution. The amount that he was charged with was so far in excess of reality in terms of his ever being able to pay that it was irrelevant whether they decided to or not. He returned to the mainland and promptly went back into business.

The trial of Coombes, Edwards and Voss was held under the auspices of the High Court of Admiralty at the Old Bailey before Sir James Marriott, President of the Court, on June 21st 1785. Almost a year had passed since the battle and it was summer again. From Christchurch, Lymington and Cowes the witnesses made their way to the sombre, shadowed hall where the accused faced the high benches of the President and his assessors and advisors. Of the three before the court, only Edwards was charged with murder. Coombes and Voss were charged with aiding and abetting, a lesser crime but still a capital one. These two were also charged with evasion of duty, the Board of Customs' basis for the earlier warrant. The sum in question was £94,000—each. William Parrott, noted as being at large, was tried in his absence.

Once again the Sarmons rehearsed the events of that day from the perspective of their positions as cutter captains. Hannah Sellers told them what had happened at the Haven House both before and during the battle. John Barnes, James Fly and John O'Connor, of *Orestes* described the landing in detail. Burden and Peter Davis told the court what they had seen both on the beach and later in the town. Thomas Taylor gave medical evidence.

Earlier in the month William Arnold had interviewed Davis at great length. He had received a further affadavit made by one William Nixon. It purported to incriminate a number of other people in the affair. Davis, known to have been there and whose story dovetailed closely with William Burden's, had never heard of Nixon. None of the people named had been there and Nixon's version of events didn't match Davis' recollection of reality at all. Arnold considered Davis a truthful witness, Nixon a wilful trouble-maker.

As the trial developed it became clear that there was insufficient evidence to carry the case against Edwards and Voss. Apart from Taylor, none of *Orestes'* officers were called for she was at sea. At the end of the evidence the judge and his aides retired to consider their verdict and sentence. A summary of the charge and the evidence were read to the court. Edwards and Voss were acquitted and discharged. Although it was never suggested that he had fired the shot, George Coombes was found guilty of the murder of William Allen.

Coombes' counsel, Mr. Fielding, now begged leave to address the court although it was late in the day. He argued that as the fatal shot had been fired from the land the trial should have been held at the county assize in Winchester, not before the Admiralty court at all. As the charge was outside the court's jurisdiction, and the accused could only be tried once he had, therefore, to be released. On the prosecution side the Attorney General, for the Crown, felt that this was not a proper interpretation. William Allen had received his fatal wound surrounded by water and had died at sea. A statute from the reign of Edward the Sixth allowed that, where such possible confusion occurred—if a fatal blow were struck in one county but the death occurred in another for example—the jurisdiction which applied was that where the fatality occurred. Sir James Marriott tended to concur with this view but held over execution of sentence until he had consulted with his fellow judges on the matter. Coombes was returned to Newgate.

During the months which followed William Arnold conducted his official and family business with his usual forthright diligence. His children had already been innoculated against smallpox and he was concerned about their contracting whooping cough. He was still endeavouring to gain the Board's permission to erect a new Customs House in West Cowes to obviate his at least twice daily ferry crossing of the Medina. He argued against the inefficiency of its position, the difficulty of his officers obtaining housing in East Cowes and the fact that the lease would soon be up for renewal. The Board argued that, as it had always been in East Cowes, there it should remain. They granted funds for improvements of which Arnold took full advantage.

He became more and more concerned with the continued silence from Joshua Jeans and then, in August, Streeter's name came up again. Back on the mainland, he had re-established his tobacco and snuff factory at Stanpit, between Christchurch and Mudeford. He was kept appraised of the declining progress of the hunt by Jeans. Late in July the *Dove*, a general trading boat, was stopped by a Revenue cutter whilst passing through the Solent bound for Christchurch. *Dove* was one of a number of commercial craft which operated a more or less legal and regular trade from Christchurch to other coastal ports.

WILLIAM ARNOLD'S HOUSE, COWES
The plaque refers to his son Thomas, the headmaster of Rugby School

William Thompson, the captain and Hannah Sellers son-in-law, claimed to be bound for Guernsey, approaching the coast only for provisions and water. Arnold was convinced that he was smuggling. On board were found fourteen packages of tobacco bearing marks which indicated that they had already been imported into London, legally, aboard the ship *Hazard*. Remaining in bond whilst in London, they had been re-exported to Guernsey. They were now being re-imported to avoid duty. The casks had one other distinguishing mark, the letter "S". They were seized. Streeter had purchased some tobacco legally. This was covered by a number of certificates of duty paid. He then used these again and again to cover quantities on which duty had been avoided, thus securing their passage to Christchurch from wherever they had been landed. Arnold informed the Board of this fraud in detail and the Board, in turn, requested the Collector at Southampton to investigate. What this enquiry ultimately uncovered was a far deeper level of corruption than even Arnold imagined.

On Saturday January 21st 1786, seven months to the day after his trial at the Old Bailey, George Coombes was before the court again. It provides a rather different picture to the commonly accepted view of justice in the Eighteenth century that his defence was taken so seriously. The committal, handed down by Mr. Justice Wilks and read in full that day, explained the reasoning behind the court's decision. William Allen had died at sea, on board H.M. sloop *Orestes* and clearly within the jurisdiction of the High Court of Admiralty. He was ordered to be returned to Newgate from whence he was to be taken to Wapping and hanged. His body was then to be hung in chains on the nearby shore, either north or south, as a warning and reminder. As an afterthought this was altered so that his cadaver could be used for anatomy instruction. In fact neither fate awaited it.

The same day an order was passed to the Governor of Newgate from the Admiralty office. It included a warrant for the execution of Coombes to be carried out on the following Monday. Beneath the secretary's signature was a postscript, signed by the President of the Court, requesting return of the warrant so that it could be properly filed.

At a little after mid-day on January 23rd 1786 George Coombes was taken under escort from Newgate to Wapping. With him went the officers of the court whose duty it was to see justice done and the order carried out. The silver oar mace, the symbol of the authority of the Admiralty, was carried before the cart in which Coombes, hands bound, was transported. A priest travelled with him. Coombes showed no sign of the terror which possessed him and behaved in a manner which gained the sympathy of many of the onlookers, including the newspaper correspondents who reported to the Hampshire Chronicle and the Salisbury and Winchester Journal. Thus those who knew him learned that he had died bravely.

His body was not taken along the coast to be hung in chains, neither was it dissected in the interests of science. Instead, by another change of instruction, it was taken in its coffin by hired wagon, regardless of winter and the appalling roads, back down the route he had travelled as a prisoner nearly a year past. Transport by cutter would have taken too long. The following day it was displayed in an iron cage, slung from a specially erected gibbet, a few yards from the Haven House at Mudeford.

That same night it was cut down by his friends, carried a short way through the forest and secretly buried.

5

"Unworthy of Any Further Trust"

The execution of George Coombes for the murder of William Allen was by no means a satisfactory end to the affair. Apart from the fact that he was known not to have pulled the trigger and that five of those wanted were still at liberty and untried, a number of other matters had emerged which William Arnold and the Board of Customs needed to clear up.

Throughout the winter of 1785 to 1786, the Collector at Southampton continued his investigation into Streeter's activities. Gradually a picture emerged of the way his tobacco business was operated, illegal importation, his suppliers and contacts and his misuse of duty certificates. As long ago as 1779 he had come to the attention of the authorities over the seizure of his first *Phoenix* and the threatening stance he had taken in an effort to recover it. The ship had been cut out of Christchurch harbour on the suspicion of the mate of the *Rose* Revenue cutter and found to have a second cargo of spirits beneath the legal one of grain. Streeter complained that the seizure was illegal and promised action in the courts if his property was not restored to him. He learned the hard way that the Board of Customs did not appreciate threats. *Phoenix* was condemned for sale at auction and Streeter had to buy her back.

Now, seven years later, he had reverted to the certification fraud. He reduced the risks by using vessels he did not own. For his personal smuggling activities he used hired crews and commanders. He took the greatest care to cover his tracks and to reduce his direct links with anything illegal to a level where they could be easily disguised. Suspicion was one thing, legally acceptable proof quite another. Streeter's standing in Christchurch was high. He was a respected and generous businessman providing employment, of various kinds, for a large proportion of the population. His children were growing up in the town. He was on particularly good terms with the local representatives of the Revenue services.

This, in itself, was causing concern to the investigating officers. Whilst they reasonably expected the co-operation and active assistance of Jeans, as their subordinate local officer, they received stonewalling and evasiveness. Jeans had failed to respond to any of the legitimate enquiries of the Board, Arnold or the Collector of Southampton. Neither he, nor his Riding Officers, offered information which they could have been expected to know and, indeed, were rarely available. True, their duties required that they spend much of their time in the saddle and could reasonably claim that the fewer people who knew of their movements the better their chances of being able to execute their duties successfully. Something, though, was very amiss.

Only Noyce was of any help and that was little enough. Jeans had been wary of him for years and had long before ensured that he knew as little as possible of the corruption which surrounded him.

In March 1786 the Collector at Cowes reported his suspicions to the Board. These were supported by the Southampton investigators. General-Surveyor Monday was dispatched to Christchurch with a platoon of troops to support him. He had the powers and ability to investigate whatever and wherever he chose, to call any witnesses and to act as he felt disposed. He remained in the area for two months, basing himself at Lymington so that his daily whereabouts were not common knowledge in Christchurch.

In early May he presented his report to the Board. He accused Jeans of inactivity, misconduct and gross negligence. Jeans had failed to support his officers in making legitimate seizures. He had instructed them to make false reports in their journals, not to name ships and individuals engaged in smuggling, to be elsewhere when runs were taking place, to go home and to bed instead of watching the coast. Instructions such as these had even applied on the day of the battle itself. He had gone to great lengths to ensure that, on the occasions when his officers wanted to carry out their duties, after repeated letters from Arnold and the Deputy-Collector at Lymington, their efforts were almost totally negated. Monday could prove all this. He was also less than satisfied with the behaviour of three of the Riding Officers, Bursey, Newsam and Reeks. He charged them with collusion, accepting bribes, aiding and abetting smuggling. All the details of the activities of the Christchurch Revenue officers during the incident at Mudeford were outlined and, again, were provable. Jeans' days were numbered.

The Board deliberated on the report throughout May. The charges were extremely serious but Jeans had, on paper at least, a fair record. He had been in the service for many years as had members of his family before him. He was a pillar of local society. In the end there was little choice. On May 30th the Collector at Southampton was instructed to call upon Jeans and Riding Officer Bursey, taking with him whatever support he felt appropriate, and to cancel their commissions and orders. These were to be returned to the Board at the end of the month with the usual accounts. Both the officers concerned were "deemed unworthy of any further trust and have therefore been dismissed".

Newsam and Reeks were not dismissed, their cases not having been proved to the Board's satisfaction. In reality this was only a legal quibble. The Board, along with its local officers, was very suspicious of them. They were warned that their conduct and activity was under close scrutiny from that point on.

Streeter watched these events with increasing alarm. He had no way of knowing if any of the officers had given information that could harm him. Early in June Supervisor Arnand from Titchfield was transferred to Christchurch, with one of his Riding Officers, to act as temporary replacements. Two weeks later they arrested John Streeter for smuggling.

Streeter, and Henry White who was arrested with him, now discovered that such warrants only lapsed if the Board decided not to pursue them. Because of their continued activities on such a large scale—and largely due to Arnold's diligence and perseverence—the Board had decided otherwise. Streeter and White were transferred to Winchester gaol to await trial.

The authorities now moved rapidly against Streeter's associates and other known smugglers, only to discover that all had not been resolved with the dismissal of Jeans. Within a few days of Streeter's arrest, Arnand moved against John Earley, who was now the leading figure amongst the smugglers. Fearing that Earley would simply take over the vacant businesses, as well as continuing his own, the new Supervisor organised an armed raid, supported by troops and his own officers. Word leaked out. Knowing that information of what he intended was being taken to Earley, he rode off to beat the informers and make the arrest himself. The troops could not be brought up quickly enough and Arnand found himself alone on enemy territory, surrounded by Earley's gang. He had outpaced the two Riding Officers who had started with him but their sudden arrival at least gave him the opportunity to retreat. By the time the soldiers arrived, Earley had disappeared. Of the two remaining Riding Officers, one was Reeks. He and John How, who had come across from Titchfield with his Supervisor, had spent the afternoon at the fair in Christchurch. Arnand could prove nothing against Reeks, in fact the Board censured him for making time-wasting accusations. Within a week they had a more serious problem. On July 7th Streeter and White escaped from prison.

The gaoler at Winchester had distinctive views on the nature of crime. Murder and robbery, offences against individuals, he held to be abhorrent. Smuggling was in a different category. He failed to see the point of prosecuting people for sums they could never hope to pay. He shared the general opinion that no one was hurt by running contraband. The prisoners, therefore, were kept in the least secure part of the gaol and the watch over them was less than complete. Although, later, no proof was offered that the gaoler had acted negligently, let alone actively helped their escape, there were rumours that sums of money had changed hands. Both escapees were men of some wealth.

Once out, they made for the coast as expected. The Board need not have worried. Both of them had learned that, without their previous protection, the game was too difficult. With their remaining influence they used their contacts to obtain passage to Guernsey where they went into hiding. Neither of them troubled the Board of Customs again.

---— 6 ———

After the Battle

Although there were numerous enquiries over the next two or three years, neither Streeter nor White were re-arrested. Streeter's wife continued his legimate businesses in Christchurch. From time to time he would cross to the mainland to visit her and ensure that all was well. On one of these occasions he was recognised, although at the time it was dark and he was disguised as a woman. He avoided capture on that occasion but, realising that things had come a long way from the time when, even with warrants out for him, he could openly carry on his activities, he slipped back across the Channel. His visits became less and less frequent. His tobacco and snuff businesses were managed by John Early who maintained them against his possible return and made sure that he always had funds available.

Times were changing. The Navy made more ships available to support the Revenue services, who now owned and manned their own fleet of cutters. Supervisors and Deputy-Collectors now called on the support of the army much more frequently, and got it. In the public's estimation smuggling had got out of hand. This was reflected in greater numbers of arrests and convictions. Local men were rarely employed as Revenue Officers in their own areas and the Board took more care to ensure their honesty. Altogether, it was getting more difficult to make a safe profit from smuggling. Between 1784 and 1789 the rates of duty were more than halved and this, more than everything else combined, caused the trade to decline. But it never quite died out.

In 1793 Britain declared war on revolutionary France. Naval support for the Revenue services ceased almost overnight and duties were increased. All along the coast men renewed old contacts and ships re-commenced the patterns of trade which brought in the contraband. More of the Government's revenue, though, now came from different sources—income and window taxes. In 1803 Napoleon Bonaparte began to build up troop concentrations on the north coast of France and acquire the hundreds of barges necessary to take them to England. In gradually but steadily increasing numbers ship owners offered their vessels and services as privateers to patrol the coast. There was a common enemy at last. Preventing Napoleon's plans was of greater importance than making a run. The threat lasted for two years, until Trafalgar in October 1805 finally destroyed the French fleet and made invasion impossible. During those years there were no recorded acts of smuggling. Half-way through, in 1804, the Government offered a general amnesty and quashed outstanding warrants. In that year John Streeter came home.

From then on he began to rebuild his life in Christchurch, buying property and managing his legal businesses. He was a free man, too old to be threatened by the navy's press or the army's crimp. He ended his days on October 28th 1824, in the house he owned next to the Ship in Distress in Stanpit. Two of his children survived him. He was seventy-four years old.

There is no record of the later lives of May or Parrott, although they might both have lived to gain the amnesty and become privateers. Likewise, there is no trace of Burden, Davis, Bursey, Reeks or Noyce. Joshua Jeans died on November 23rd 1786, broken by events which had led to his dismissal and no longer as respected in the town. One of his sons became a doctor.

Christchurch itself was changing. Already there had been much interest shown in improving the harbour for legal trade. Twenty-two years before the Battle of Mudeford, John Smeaton, who designed the Eddystone Lighthouse, had been commissioned to prepare plans although these had not been implemented. This was principally due to those who felt that improvements would make smuggling more difficult. Now this interest was beginning to re-appear. Christchurch breweries supplied shiploads of beer to the navy throughout the French wars. Communications were gradually improving with the spread of the turnpikes and Christchurch was not now so isolated. The reduction in duties after the end of the war in 1815 led to the terminal decline of the old ways of smuggling. On Bourne Heath the first tentative developments which led to the growth of the resort of Bournemouth were already beginning, under the inspiration of Lewis Tregonwell. He had held command of the troops on the coast, principally in support of the Revenue services, between 1796 and 1802. Military barracks were established in Christchurch itself in 1795. Within a decade of Streeter's death there was talk of a new harbour at Christchurch—for pleasure craft. Having seen out the American Revolution and the great French wars, Streeter lived to hear of the first steamships and railways. He died in a different world.

His chief opponent, William Arnold, had remained Collector at Cowes to the end of his days. He never saw the new Customs House in the western part of the town. He died on March 5th 1801, aged fifty-five. Deeply respected by his employers, associates and even enemies, he was worn out by his service. His son, Thomas, went on to become Headmaster of Rugby School.

The Sarmon family continued to provide commanders for the Revenue cutters even after the contract system was absorbed. George Sarmon gave up command of *Swan* to his brother Francis in 1786. Francis, who had sailed as midshipman with Lt. Crook in the *Expedition*, was still in command when she was wrecked near Shoreham in 1792. He went on to command two more *Swans*, one a converted smuggler, between 1793 and 1795, when it was captured by the French but its officers released. The following year, whilst commanding the purpose-built cutter of the same name, he tangled with a more powerful French privateer, and in the ensuing fight was killed. James continued to command the *Resolution* Excise cutter until 1786 when she was transferred to Hull. She was broken up in 1800.

Little is recorded of *Orestes* people, apart from her Commander and First Lieutenant. When she paid-off in May 1786 Ellis left her, although Francis Ross remained as senior, staying with her during her transfer to the Channel station where she served until 1793. When *Orestes* was ordered to the Leeward Islands, Francis Ross was made First Lieutenant in *Tremendous* (74), a ship-of-the-line. She was part of Lord Howe's squadron involved in blockading the French north coast ports. At the end of May 1794 the squadron fought the escorting ships of a huge French grain convoy. The convoy escaped but so much damage was done to its escort that the battle became known as "The Glorious First of June". On that day Francis Ross was killed in action.

James Ellis continued to serve the Admiralty in administrative roles until the year after Trafalgar when he retired. He received an out-pension of Greenwich Hospital from September 22nd 1806. He lived for a further eighteen years, dying at the age of seventy-nine on September 7th 1824, six weeks before Streeter.

Orestes herself returned from the Leeward Islands and was actually attached to Howe's fleet in June 1794. She was employed in the Channel for the next few years. In September 1797, under the command of Captain Parker, she captured a large French privateer, *Le Furet*, off Portland. In the following year she was part of the squadron which captured Diamond Rock in the approaches to St. Vaast. In fact this was one of the St. Marcou islets which was taken by Sir William Sydney Smith of the frigate *Diamond*, armed with ships guns and used to provide a solid fortress from which to prevent use of the roadstead. *Orestes* helped to beat off attempts to recapture it. On July 9th, still under the command of William Haggitt, she was ordered to the East Indies station.

In October she was sighted and spoken to by H.M. frigate *Hebe* and, at the beginning of November, by a homeward-bound East Indiaman who warned her of a storm developing on her track. On November 5th 1799, over-whelmed by a hurricane, *Orestes* foundered with the loss of all her people.

—— 7 ——

Postscript

With the passing of the principal participants, the "Battle of Mudeford" faded in to that mixture of half-remembered truths and myth which forms the legend of the smugglers.

The places in which the story developed began to change. In 1823 the Haven House was taken over by the Revenue service as a preventive station and extended to provide better accommodation. A new public house, of the same name, was built a little further to landward along the spit. In the early 1860s cottages to house coastguards and their families were built alongside the old inn. During the 1850s and 60s, George Holloway, a local coal and lime merchant, began mining the ironstone on Hengistbury Head. In doing so he removed the Head's natural defence against the sea and the result radically changed the form of the harbour entrance. The arrival of the railway in the same decade began the decline in seabourne trade, which had effectively ceased by the early years of the Twentieth century. Christchurch has expanded in size by almost thirty times since 1784.

Cowes, too, has changed. It was badly bombed in 1942, destroying many of the old landmarks. Like Christchurch, it has expanded rapidly and changed considerably in character.

Of the events of 1784, apart from the documentation stored in various archives around the country, there are few tangible remains. Yet there are some. At Mudeford, the Haven House still stands and in the town, 10 Bridge Street used to contain Jeans' office. The Priory, castle and Constable's house with their surrounding pattern of medieval streets, would still be recognisable. The site of the summer house on Hengistbury Head is now occupied by the Coastguard lookout. At Stanpit, the Sea-scouts' headquarters is T.S. *Orestes*. The building which probably contained Streeter's tobacco manufactory still stands as does the Ship in Distress.

In Cowes, Arnold's house is still there although the Customs House and quay have gone. There is a monument to him in Whippingham Church. St. Mary's Church in Cowes is much altered but still contains a monument to Francis Sarmon. In the graveyard, surrounded by bushes and beneath closely mown grass, lies the man who this story is really all about, William Allen, Master of the *Orestes* and shot by smugglers at Christchurch.

MONUMENT TO FRANCIS SARMON
in St. Mary's Church, Cowes

TOMBSTONE OF WILLIAM ALLEN
in St. Mary's Churchyard, Cowes

Appendix 1

LETTER FROM WILLIAM ARNOLD, COLLECTOR OF CUSTOMS AT COWES, REGARDING THE PROBLEMS AND METHODS OF SMUGGLING AND OFFERING SUGGESTIONS TO REDUCE THEM.

Customs House,
Cowes,
23rd Oct. 1783.

To Custom House,
London.

Honourable Sirs,

In obedience to your order of the 11th inst. we beg leave to report that smuggling within the last three years has increased upon this coast to an alarming degree and the illicit trade is principally carried on in large armed cutters or luggers from two or three hundred tons burden, with which the Revenue Cruisers are not able to contend, insomuch that it is no unusual thing for them to land their goods in open day under the protection of their guns, and sometimes in sight of Revenue Cutters, whom they will not suffer to come near or board them.

The warfare gave sanction to the arming of these vessels, as the Masters took out Commissions as Privateers, tho in fact they followed no other trade than smuggling and notwithstanding the war is now at an end, they continue their illicit practices.

Armed and in great force these vessels frequently convoy over other smaller ones and keep off at sea till towards night, then they run in and land their cargoes, the larger vessels at places where the gangs of smugglers sometimes to the number of 200 or 300 are previously appointed to meet them, and the smaller vessels at such other places on the shore where they can bury the goods on the beach, deposit them in cellars or sink them near the shore till opportunity offers of removing them again.

Goods are also frequently landed out of large deep boats, carrying from 500 to 1,000 casks which have been unshipped at sea from importing vessels, who as soon as they are seen or chased by a Revenue Cutter drop the boat astern, which immediately rowed-off, whilst the Commander of the Revenue Cutter is pursuing the vessel, he supposes to be loaded, but when he comes up with, he to his great disappointment finds has no cargo on board.

We humbly submit to your Honours' consideration, whether if the Hovering Act was extended to three leagues off the coast, it might be some check to the present practice of smuggling, as it would keep the smuggling vessels during the day at a greater distance from the coast and render their landing goods or arriving at the appointed time on the shore more hazardous and uncertain.

To such a regular sinecure is smuggling now reduced, that we are informed that the smugglers have stated prices for their goods in proportion to the distance they bring them.

If they sell any at sea to coasting or small vessels or boats, the price of a 4 Gall. cask of brandy is about half a Guinea, or 11 shillings. If landed on the shore between Hurst and Christchurch, under the protection of their guns and put into quick possession of the land smugglers, 14 to 15 shillings a cask, and if brought within the Isle of Wight or to Langston or Portsmouth the price advances to a Guinea a cask, according to the Place at which it is to be landed or delivered.

Our enquiries have furnished us with the following list of Smuggling vessels which carry on their illicit trade between the Needles and Peveral Point.

THE CORNISH RANGER—Wallard, belonging to Causand, A Lugger of about 300 tons Mounting 26 guns. Frequently lands goods between the Needles and Christchurch Head and no longer ago than the 21st or 30th of Sept. landed 3,000 casks of Foreign spirits and 10 or 12 tons of tea, and at the same time brought over under her convoy 3 other Luggers.

THE WASP—Hall of Folkestone, Built at Cowes 270 tons 22 guns, works between the Needles and Christchurch.

THE JOHN AND SUSANNA—Andrew Hague of Folkestone, built at Cowes, same burden and force and frequents the same spot.

The beforementioned vessels carry from 60 to 80 men and smuggle upon an average each trip from two to 3,000 casks and 8 or 10 tons of tea. If they go to Guernsey they return about once a fortnight, if to Dunkerque once in 3 weeks.

Besides the above a new cutter is now fitting out here and nearly ready for sea; she is called the FAVOURITE belongs to one Sturges of Hamble, a noted smuggler. Is the burden of 220 tons to mount 20 guns and it is supposed is intended to smuggle this coast.

Hurst Castle is a place of great rendezvous for smugglers and in its neighbourhood are several smaller Luggers which land goods between Hurst and Christchurch and frequently supply the smugglers at the West part of the Isle of Wight. One of these Luggers THE PHOENIX about 90 to 100 tons burden belonging to one Streeter, a noted smuggler but of which one May was late Master, has this week been brought into this Port by the Master of the King's Cutter, the cruiser with a small quantity of Brandy and tea on board, having before landed, as is supposed the principal part of her cargo near Hurst-Christchurch.

Open boats or Shallops, lugger rigged, have frequently been built here of 70 foot in length and carry from 500 to 1,000 casks with which they draw but little water they can with great facility run ashore upon the beach where the gangs are upon the shore ready to receive and carry away the goods.

Besides these there are many rowing boats 40ft. long and upwards, tho apparently made to row with only 6 oar, yet are so constructed that by means of shifting Thwarts and other contrivances they can row with 10 or 12 oars. As these kinds of boats when seized and condemned are generally broke up and produce little or nothing to the seizing Officer, we apprehend they are not so assiduous in looking after and seizing them when not loaded, as they perhaps might be if a premium or bounty was allowed to the seizing officer for every foot of length of boats seized under those circumstances.

And we humbly apprehend if the building these kind of boats except for His Majesty's service was restrained to a certain length, perhaps 25ft. it would prevent them rowing with the number they now do, and boats in the Revenue Service would stand a better chance of coming up with them.

We beg leave to submit to your Honour as our opinion that unless some effectual measures are adopted to suppress the LARGE CLASS of smuggling vessels now used and to prevent them going ARMED smuggling will still increase, for where so large a property is at stake they naturally run greater risques to protect it, and of course become more daring and desperate, and carry on their fraudulant trade in defiance of the law and all the efforts of the Officers to prevent them.

With respect to increasing the number of Officers at this Port further than with the Cutter and boat crews, whom your Honours have lately agreed to employ here, we do not know that at present it is necessary. Stationing a Frigate with a King's Cutter in Studland Bay and a King's Cutter also in Hurst Road may probably be of service for the Revenue Cruisers occasionally to resort to for assistance.

And if they only serve to keep off the large cutters from landing their goods for 3 to 4 days at a time, when the large gangs of land smugglers are appointed to meet them on the shore. It would go far, we apprehend to ruin the trade, because the expense of keeping so large a number of men and horses collected together waiting the arrival of goods, must very materially diminish the profits arising from the sale of them, which is Humbly submitted by

W.A. (William Arnold)

I.R.

Appendix 2

COMMANDER'S LOG ENTRIES, H.M. SLOOP-OF-WAR *ORESTES*, JULY 15TH AND 16TH. THE DAYS OF THE RUN AND THE BATTLE OF MUDEFORD

Thursday 15th. Wind NE then SW.
Position at Noon Needles NE, distance 4 miles.

Moderate and clear, at 8p.m. weighed and stood eastward. From 10p.m. to 3a.m. cruising between Bourne and Whitepit. At half past 3 stood on eastward and at 6 anchored in Freshwater Bay in 9 fathoms. At 11 weighed and stood westward.

Friday 16th. Wind variable and calms.
Position at Noon Christchurch, NE distance 3 miles.

Light breezes and calms. From 3 to 5p.m. lying-too off Poole Bar in company with the Excise and *Swan* revenue cutters. At half past 5 stood eastward and at 6 sent our boats, manned and armed (as did the cutters) into Christchurch Harbour to bring out two smuggling luggers that had landed their cargoes the day before.

When the boats approached the vessels, they were fired upon by the smugglers, both from the luggers and two houses. The boats continuing their approach, the smugglers left their vessels, when our people boarded them, but finding the luggers both aground, the smugglers keeping up a constant fire and growing dark, occasioned our boats to return, bringing on board Mr. W. Allen (Master) mortally wounded and a marine shot through the arm. Fired several shots from th' brig and cutters. At 3a.m. being calm, towed the cutters inshore, got springs on their cables and sent the boats on board the smugglers, where finding no opposition, towed them out of the harbour. At 6a.m. departed this life Mr. William Allen, Master.

Appendix 3

WILLIAM ARNOLD'S REPORT TO THE BOARD OF CUSTOMS CONCERNING THE INCIDENT AT MUDEFORD, JULY 20TH 1784

Custom House, Cowes
20th July 1784.

To: Custom House,
London.   No. 88

Hon. Sirs,

On the 16th inst. Two large Lugsail vessels were brought into this Port by the Officers of the *Orestes* Sloop of War having been seized in Christchurch Harbour by them, in conjunction with Mr. James Sarmon Commander of an Excise Revenue Cutter and Mr. George Sarmon Commander of the *Swan* Cutter in the service at this Port for having the preceeding day unlawfully imported and run a large quantity of tea and foreign spirits near Christchurch Head within the limits of the Port of Southampton.

We are sorry to acquaint your Honours that the Officers were oppos'd, obstructed and wantonly fired upon when rowing into Christchurch Harbour and before they had landed or taken possession of the vessels by a number of smugglers assembled on board the Lugger and on the shore. Mr. Allen, Master of the *Orestes* and who also acted under a Deputation from your Honours was shot and is since dead and one of the Mariners wounded in the arm. An inquest has been taken on the body of Mr. Allen. The jury having returned a verdict of Wilful Murder, the Coroner has issued warrants for apprehending William Parrott and William May, two persons who were proved to have been accessories in the Murder; none of the rest are yet known or discovered. A transaction of this kind having happened in the face of the day, and so near Christchurch it is more than probable that many of the persons assembled on the spot must be known in the neighbourhood especially as the smugglers sheltered themselves in a Public House called the Haven House, from the windows of which, and the stable adjoining, several muskets were fired at the Officers.

We have judged it necessary to write to Mr. Jeans, Supervisor of the Riding Officers at Christchurch, to excite him to use his endeavours to

55

apprehend the offenders and to transmit any information he may collect that is likely to lead to a discovery of any of Persons concerned in the Murder.

Never was a more unprovoked attack made on Officers of the Revenue than in the present instance and it shows how necessary exemplary punishment is for such daring violators of the Law.

The smugglers had not even the pretence to urge of firing in their own defence, for many shots were fired on the Officers from behind sand banks and sheltered places and Mr. Allen who was first wounded in the thigh and afterwards in the body received his death wound before a single gun was fired by the Revenue Officers.

A report having gone abroad that before the intended Act for preventing of smuggling takes place, an Act of oblivion for all smuggling offences will also be passed, we are fully persuaded they are induced to act in a more daring and desparate manner under an idea (but a mistaken one we hope) that all offences against the Revenue or outrages on Officers will be pardoned.

From the very great numbers concerned (as the Officers report) in this business, we are humbly of the opinion that if Pardon and a reward was offered to any of the persons so unlawfully assembled except those who actually fired or killed the Officer, it might lead to arrest of the most atrocious offenders.

Inclosed we transmit to you two lists found on board one of the vessels, they contain the names of many persons known to be noted smugglers. The Officers were repeatedly fired upon from persons on board the vessels, tho they all quitted scuttled and carried away the sails before the officers could get up to the beach, where they were run on shore. It is but reasonable to suppose the persons belonged to them were some of those concerned.

We submit to your Honours whether it will not be sufficient for advertising and apprehending them on suspicion. At any rate we hope your Honours will order such steps to be taken as you may think most likely to bring the offenders to justice.

The Vessels under seizure were seen the preceeding day employed in landing a very large quantity of tea and foreign spirits which were carried off between two and three o'clock in the afternoon by upwards of 50 wagons and two or three hundred horses, but the smugglers would not suffer W. Sarmon of the Excise Cutter who fell in with them at the time either to go on board the vessels or take away any of the goods which were on the shore.

He stood to sea again and meeting with the *Orestes* and *Swan* Cutter they joined and went in pursuit of the vessels which they seized as before mentioned.

We are your Honours most humble and obedient servants.

W.A.

I.R.

Appendix 4

ENTRY IN THE REGISTER OF BURIALS FOR COWES, JULY 19TH 1784 AND FROM THE SALISBURY AND WILTSHIRE JOURNAL, JULY 26TH 1784 RECORDING THE FUNERAL OF WILLIAM ALLEN

1784. July 19. William Allen aged 25 years. Master of y *Orestes* & shot by Smugglers at Christchurch.

July 26th 1784.

On Monday evening last, was brought on shore and buried here the body of the unfortunate Master of the *Orestes* who was mortally wounded in the engagement with the smugglers last week at Christchurch.

He was attended to the grave by the whole ship's crew, the officers supporting the pall, accompanied by a party of marines, who preceeded the corpse, with their arms reversed, amidst a greater concourse of people than was ever known, who with tears lamented the untimely death of such a fine young man, who was universally respected by his fellow officers, and revered by the whole ship's crew. He had just entered the 25th year of his age.

Appendix 5

LETTER FROM WILLIAM ARNOLD TO THE BOARD OF CUSTOMS CONCERNING THE ARREST OF BONE TUCKER AND GUERNSEY JEMMY

To Custom House,   Custom House, Cowes.
London.   No. 12   3rd Jan. 1785

Hon. Sirs,

Pursuant to your order of the 5th inst. No. 3. Bone Tucker, one of the persons detained on suspicion of being concerned in the late outrage and Murder committed by the smugglers at Christchurch, has been carried before a Magistrate for examination.

But it not appearing by the evidence on the part of the Crown that Tucker neither fired nor was in any degree aiding, assisting or encouraging those who did fire, but that he left the vessel on the approach of the Revenue boats, and went from the place immediately as the firing began. Tucker himself proving that in his haste to get away he left his clothes behind, and was met on his way to Christchurch at the time the smugglers were firing.

The Magistrates did not think the evidence sufficient to commit upon and he was accordingly set at liberty.

With respect to Guernsey Jemmy, the other person detained on suspicion, he found means to escape from the Excise Cutter where he was confined, before your order for taking him before a Magistrate was received, there being reason to suspect that he escaped if not by the connivance at least through the negligence and inattention of those who had charge of him.

The Collector has desired the Tide Surveyor of Excise who himself has shown great zeal and activity through the whole of the business, to report the misconduct of his Officers to the Board of Excise, who we trust will at least express their disapprobation of the conduct of such of them as appear to have been culpable on this occasion.

We beg leave further to acquaint you that a warrant is issued to retake Guernsey Jemmy in case he can be found, in order that he can be properly examined before the Magistrate.

The Collector doubts if at present he is in possession of such evidence against him, as would induce any Magistrate to commit him for trial.

We are your Honours most obedient and humble servants.

W.A.

I.R.

Appendix 6

THE INFORMATION OF WILLIAM BURDEN OF LYMINGTON IN THE COUNTY OF HANTS. MARINER. TAKEN UPON OATH THE 20TH AUG. 1784

Saith,

That John Streeter of Christchurch having been applied to by the informant in the Month of July last (being then out of employ) for a berth, Streeter ordered informant to go on board the *Civil Usage* Lugger, Commanded by William May then lying in Christchurch Road that there was no agreement for wages. Informant accordingly went on board. The crew consisted of about thirty persons, including Officers. The Lugger went out of Christchurch Road in Ballast to Hurst Road for shelter. There she stayed one night, and from thence went to Guernsey where she took in some Liquor and Teas, and proceeded from thence to Alderney where she took in more Liquor and Teas.

She came out from thence and was chased back by a Cutter (supposed to belong to the Custom House) into Alderney Road, laid there about three hours and then sailed for Cherbourg, and waited there several days. Sailed from thence in the Morning for the North Shore and was chased back by the *Rose* Cutter to Cherbourg, where they put all the goods in the Store Houses, and came over to Christchurch in one or two days in Ballast. The Boat belonging to the *Rose* Cutter immediately upon their arrival (that was about one or two o'clock in the morning) boarded them. Informant and Peter Davis another of the Lugger's Crew then left the Lugger and went home to Lymington. On the 14th, the day after Davis and Informant left the Lugger, they returned together to Christchurch for the clothes that were left on board, having been advised to quit the service.

They learnt she had sailed from there the night before or later that morning. That Davis and Informant stayed at Christchurch that night, and about two or three o'clock in the afternoon of the next day the Informant and Davis went on board the Lugger which came in there Loaded, in company with another which was also Loaded.

Both Luggers landed their goods without interruption.

That Davis and Informant both assisted in towing the Casks and carrying the Tea on shore from on board. That they also assisted to haul the Luggers into Christchurch Harbour.

After the goods were landed, before the Luggers had got into the Harbour, a boat from an Excise Cutter hailed them and asked to go on board.

Knows not what answer was given, informant then being at a considerable distance, tracking the Luggers into the Harbour.

That upon the Luggers being moored in the Harbour, informant and Davis left them and went into the Town, where they slept together at the house of William Burden, a fisherman.

Next morning William May, the Captain of the Lugger to which Davis and informant belonged came to them and asked them to help to Ballast the Luggers, that they consenting and after finishing Ballasting, returned on shore with William Webb, Henry Tross, Joseph Seven, George Bond and Bone Tucker and went to the house of Mrs. Sellers upon Haven Point. Soon afterwards the *Orestes* sloop and two or three Cutters came in sight.

John Streeter came to Mrs. Seller's house on horse back and ordered informant and the other persons that were in the house, to assist in getting the sails off the Luggers on shore.

They thereupon assisted and several of the sails were carried into out-houses of Mrs. Sellers and one Mr. Wheeler.

During which time some of the cutter's boats came near to the shore. Mr. Parrott Capt. of the Lugger in company with one in which Informant sailed, fired a musket or Blunderbuss at the crew of the Cutter's boats before they fired at all.

William May, Informant's Captain, also fired a musket or Blunderbuss several times at the Crew of the Cutter's boats but cannot say whether it was before or after they fired. William Harris who belonged to Parrott's Lugger fired several times.

That the boat's crew were about 200 yards off at the time of the firing according to the best of Informant's judgement.

Knows not what the Musket and Blunderbuss were loaded with. When firing began informant got into a Bedroom in Mrs. Seller's House and after five or six muskets or Blunderbusses were fired.—From there upon the bank to Christchurch where they stayed with Henry Tros, Geo. Bond and Peter Davis till the firing was over and the men returned from the beach.

That May came by them on horses back towards Christchurch and said 'O you Cowards—You Cowards''. That he soon returned with a small cask under his left arm which Informant apprehended contained ammunition for firing.

That the firing was much more frequent after his return than what it was during his absence.

That May and Parrot were the last to leave the beach. That William Harris and David Bell were the only persons Informant saw firing at the Cutter's boat.

William Burden.

Appendix 7

THE SENTENCE OF THE HIGH COURT OF ADMIRALTY ON GEORGE COOMBES, JONATHAN EDWARDS AND HENRY VOSS, JUNE 21ST 1785

High Court of Admiralty for our Lord the King Upon their Oath. That

William Parrott late of London, labourer
Jonathan Edwards late of London, labourer
Henry Voss otherwise Noss, late of London, labourer
George Coombes late of London, labourer
William May late of London, labourer
John Cooper late of London, labourer
William Harris late of London, labourer
Joseph Savon late of London, labourer
David Bull late of London, labourer.

And divers other persons whose names are as yet unknown. To the said knaves not having the fear of God before their eyes but being moved and seduced by the instigation of the Devil.

On the 14th day of July in the 24th year of our Sovereign Lord George III, King of Great Britain, with force and arms on the high seas and in the Jurisdiction of the Admiralty of England, about the distance of half a mile from Christchurch Harbour in the County of Southampton, In and upon William Allen in the Peace of God and our said Lord the King, felloniously, wilfully and with malice aforethought did make an assault, and the said William Parrott with a certain gun to the value of five shillings then and there charged with gunpowder and one leaden bullet, which gun he the said William Parrott in both his hands then and there did feloniously wilfully and with malice aforethought discharge and shoot upon the said William Allen—and that the said William Parrott then and there by the fire of the gunpowder did strike and wound William Allen in and upon the thigh and upon the right side of the belly of him the said William Allen, and did give him with a lead bullet, one mortal wound to the depth of four inches, and to the breadth of half an inch.

Of which said mortal wound, he the same William Allen from the 15th day of July in the 24th year, until the 16th day of the said month of July in the year aforesaid on the high seas within the jurisdiction of the Admiralty did languish and live on until the said 16th day of July.

George Coombes convicted of felony and Murder, judgement is respited until the opinion of all the Judges be taken in this case.

Jonathan Edwards Henry Voss Severally acquitted of felony and murder, let them be discharged.

Appendix 8

LETTER FROM THE BOARD OF CUSTOMS TO THE COLLECTOR AT SOUTHAMPTON WITH THE INSTRUCTIONS FOR THE DISMISSAL OF JOSHUA STEVENS JEANS

Customs House, London.
30th May 1786.

Gentleman.
Having read the report of Mr. Monday, one of our General Surveyors, on the several charges given by him to Mr. Joshua Steven Jeans, Supervisor of the Riding Officers at Christchurch within the limits of your Port and particularly—

That contrary to his Duty and in violation of his admission Oaths he had not supported and properly assisted the several Riding Officers under his supervision, but on the contrary had frequently discountenanced them on several occasions when in due execution of their Duty.

That when applied to by the said Officers (on their having seen many Wagons, Carts and Horsemen go through the Town to the sea side) for his aid, assistance and advice in order to take such measures as might be thought best to prevent the running of the cargoes of two Smuggling Vessels lying at anchor near the shore, the said Jeans, instead of joining the said Officers, or taking any steps to prevent the said cargoes from being run, advised the said Officers to return to their homes and go to bed.

That he had contrary to the 26th Article of the Riding Officers' Instructions, repeatedly forbad them to enter in their Journal the names and descriptions of such Vessels employed on illicit trade as they might observe in the rivers and creeks in their respective districts, particularly in July 1784 when the *Orestes* sloop of war attempted to seize two large smuggling Luggers Commanded by May and Parrott in Christchurch Harbour, when the said Jeans positively ordered the Riding Officers not to take any notice or make any remark in their Journal, of the transactions of the day although the Master of the *Orestes* was murdered by the smugglers in the execution of the before mentioned duty.

And for various other Mal practices. And having also read the said Officer's answers, the evidence of the several persons examined on this occasion and the observations of Mr. Monday thereupon.

It appears that the said Jeans has not only been negligent and inactive himself, but had discouraged and discountenanced the Officers under his supervision when disposed to do their duty, and that instead of enforcing a strict observance of the orders and instructions of this Board as specially referred to in the before-mentioned charge he repeatedly forbad them to enter in their Journals the names and descriptions of the Vessels and boats employed in illicit trade lying in the Creeks in the respective districts, even after the Officers in this district had been especially enjoined by the Collector of Cowes and Deputy Customer of Lymington strictly to attend to and observe the Board's orders on this subject.

We deem the said Jeans unworthy of any further trust in the service of the Revenue and have therefore dismissed him therefrom.

And you are to call in and cancel his commission and instructions and transmit the same hither with your next account by the carrier. And having read the charge given by Wm. Monday to William Newsam, Robert Reeks, and John Bursey Riding Officers at Christchurch. That contrary to their duty and in violation of their Oath and in breach of the 32nd Article of their instructions—

They in the Month of July 1784 at High Cliffe near Christchurch Received of John Streeter Master of the *Civil Usage* Lugger or some other of the smugglers engaged in landing the cargo of the said Lugger upwards of one hundred small casks of spirits marked (F) permitting at the same time the other part of the cargo consisting of about eight tons of tea and between two and three thousand casks of spirits to be conveyed away by the smugglers without interruption.

And having likewise read their respective answers there to, the evidence of the several persons examined on this occasion and Mr. Monday's observations upon the whole. It clearly appearing that Bursey did go down to the shore at the time the cargo of the said Lugger was landing, and enquired of the smugglers whether their (meaning the Officers') Tubs were on shore. And that after receiving the Tubs marked (F) from the smugglers, he carried the same off unmolested to the Customs House. We therefore deem him guilty of Collusion with the smugglers and consequently unworthy of any further trust in the Service of the Revenue and have therefore dismissed him therefrom.

And you are to call in and cancel his Commission and instructions and transmit the same by the carrier as before directed.

As the charges against Newsam and Reeks for Collusion are not proved, we do not proceed to inflict any punishment upon them, yet as their names appear to the Seizure and they of course benefitted thereby, the said Newsam and Reeks are liable to strong suspicion of a connivance also to this transaction, and it is therefore particularly incumbent on them by their activity and future good conduct to efface their impression and to exert themselves in the due and faithful execution of their duty.

William Hey   H. Pelham
S. Parten.   Jas. Jeffreys

Appendix 9

THE CAREERS OF JAMES ELLIS AND FRANCIS ROSS

JAMES ELLIS:

1771 Commissioned Fourth Lieutenant, H.M.S. *MARLBOUROUGH* (74), third rate ship–of–the–line.

1777 First Lieutenant, H.M. Sloop *FLY*.

1778 First Lieutenant, H.M. Frigate *ARETHUSA* (32), Capt. Marshall. Wounded in action against French frigate *BELLE POULE* (36), June 17th. Promoted Commander November 19th.

1778–9 Commander H.M. Armed Ship *PRINCESS OF WALES* (20). Stationed in North Sea.

1780–3 Commander H.M. Sloop *SCOUT* (14), brig–rigged sloop. Stationed in Irish Sea. Captured French privateer *LE GLORIEUX* (12), 1781. Paid off April 1783.

1783–6 Commander H.M. Sloop *ORESTES* (18), brig–rigged sloop. Stationed Isle of Wight and Portland. Paid off May 1786.

1806 Granted out-pension of the Royal Naval Hospital, Greenwich, September 22nd.

1824 Died September 7th.

FRANCIS ROSS:

1779 Commissioned Lieutenant, August 28th.

1782–93 First Lieutenant, H.M. Sloop *ORESTES* (18). Stationed Isle of Wight and Portland to May 1786, Channel to 1793.

1793 First Lieutenant H.M.S. *TREMENDOUS* (74), third rate ship-of-line. Killed in action June 1st 1794.

Appendix 10

DESCRIPTIONS AND CAREERS OF THE SHIPS INVOLVED AT THE BATTLE OF MUDEFORD

ORESTES:

Brig-rigged sloop-of-war. Armed with 18 nine-pounder guns (but pierced for 26). 90ft. 4in. on gundeck, 81ft. 7in. of keel, 30ft. 4in. in the beam, 12ft. depth of hold. 395 tons. Nominal complement 125 officers, men and marines.

Originally Dutch privateer *MARS* captured (in company with her confederate *HERCULES*) December 3rd 1781 off Flamborough Head by H.M. Sloop *ARTOIS*, Capt. Macbride.

Commissioned *ORESTES* June 1782. Attached to Channel squadron under Cdr. J. E. Hope-Bowers. 1783–6 Isle of Wight and Portland, Cdr. J. Ellis. 1786–92 Channel, M. Dixon (86–8), T. R. Shivers (89–90), Sir H. Burrard (90–93). To Leeward Islands 1793, Capt. Lord Augustus Fitzroy. 1794 with Howe's fleet at the "Glorious First of June", thereafter cruising Channel, Cdr. C. Parker (96–98). Captured French privateer *LE FURET* September 3rd 1797. Under W. Haggitt assisted in repulse of attack on St. Marcou Islets, May 6th 1798. July 9th sailed for East Indies. Lost with all hands in a hurricane November 5th 1799.

SWAN:

English Customs Cutter. Armed with 10 six-pounder guns. Built Broadstairs by Thomas White, January 1784. 90 tons. Complement 25 officers and men. Contract vessel built to the orders of, and contracted to, William Arnold, Collector of Customs at Cowes. Commanded by George Sarmon to 1786, thereafter Francis Sarmon. Bought by service when contract completed January 5th 1788. Refitted London 1788–9. Stationed for whole career at Cowes, Isle of Wight. Wrecked near Shoreham May 26th 1792.

RESOLUTION:

English Excise Cutter. Armed with 8 four-pounder guns. Built 1781. 103 tons. Complement 18 officers and men. Stationed Cowes 1781–90. Commanded by James Sarmon 1784–6, thereafter P. Stoneham. Transferred to Hull 1790, Ilfracombe 1798. Broken-up 1800.

CIVIL USAGE:

Lugger, coastal trader. Pierced for 20–22 six-pounder guns. length of keel 77ft., beam 14ft. 2in. Built 1784. 73 tons. Clinker built. Owned by J. Streeter. A new ship having completed one voyage under W. May when seized July 1784. No further details.

PHOENIX:

Lugger, coastal trader. Pierced for 22 six-pounder guns. Length of keel 90ft., beam 15ft. 96 tons. Clinker built. Owned by J. Streeter. Approximately two years old when seized July 16th 1784. No further details.

Appendix 11

RIGGING AND GUNNERY

The term "sloop" had a different meaning in the Eighteenth century. It was applied to small warships of up to 26 guns with open gun-decks and two or three masts. Below 12 guns they were commanded by Lieutenants, above that figure they had a Commander. Vessels above 28 guns were classed as frigates and were commanded by Captains.

The term "brig-sloop" meant that the vessel carried square sails on two masts. Three masts would have made her a "ship". The top-gallant masts were the third, or uppermost section of the masts. The length of spars was determined by the size of the trees available. Masts were usually built in three or four sections.

A "cutter" carried only one mast, rigged fore and aft, like a modern yacht. Two triangular sails were carried between the mast and the bowsprit, a large gaff (four sided) sail behind the mast. Above this there was usually a gaff topsail and, sometimes, there were square sails as well.

"Luggers" carried sails on two or three masts. These sails were arranged so that one-third was ahead of the mast, two-thirds behind it. They were set as fore and aft sails, not across the breeze. Small luggers sometimes had "dipping" sails which could be set either side of the mast but larger luggers had "standing" sails, so they sailed better on one tack than the other where the sail pressed against the mast. As far as the hulls were concerned, they were similar to other vessels of equivalent size.

Most sloops-of-war were armed with six-pounder guns, cutters with four- or six-pounders. *Orestes* had nine-pounders because that was her armament when captured. At the time of the battle all would have been "long-guns" for maximum range. Depending on the quality of the gun, ball, gunner and sea state their range was up to a mile, sometimes more, with reasonable accuracy for half that distance. Ammunition consisted of a round shot of iron weighing four, six or nine pounds, depending on the gun. The charge was gunpowder in a pre-filled, cloth cartridge-bag. The weight of the charge varied slightly, sometimes deliberately, as did the quality of the powder. No two rounds were quite alike.

Stories of shot hitting the Priory are unlikely. The distance is too great and the direction is wrong. Likewise, tales of chain-shot striking the Haven House. Chain-shot consisted of two round-shot linked by a metre of chain. They were expensive and inaccurate. Their proper function was to destroy the enemy's rigging and render them out of control. *Civil Usage* and *Phoenix* were not only aground but had had their masts removed to prevent their seizure. Cheaper and more accurate, round-shot would almost certainly have been used.

Appendix 12

NOTES ON THE SOURCES

As far as possible, this story has been compiled from primary sources, that is those written by people involved in the events, often from the original documents. Most of the principal documents are held at the Public Record Office at Kew or, in the case of the High Court of Admiralty documents, Chancery Lane. Many of the remainder are held at the National Maritime Museum or the County Record Offices at Newport (Isle of Wight), Dorchester (Dorset) and Winchester (Hampshire). A few are held at the Red House Museum (Christchurch) and the Cowes Maritime Museum (Isle of Wight).

Newspaper sources are kept at their respective County Record Offices whilst most of the unpublished secondary material is kept at the Cowes Maritime Museum and the National Maritime Museum, where most of the published material is also available.

Whilst the Battle of Mudeford is particularly well-documented, there are gaps. Where contemporary secondary sources are available these have been used, except where they contradict primary material. In the case of letters, it is regretably rare to come across both query or report and reply. The principal reason for this is the destruction of archives by enemy action during the Second World War. By taking account of known action under similar circumstances most of the gaps may be filled with a fair degree of probability. Account has been taken of the capabilities of the ships and communication systems at the time. All dates and names have been checked against contemporary sources. The evidence at Coombes' trial was not recorded but the names of the witnesses were.

The characters of Parrott and Coombes have been developed from the common threads of other stories in which they, or characters representing them, appear.

One should always be careful when considering events outside personal experience. These events have been recorded as accurately as it is possible to be two centuries later.

Sources

Primary Sources

Public Record Office:

ADM 12/54 Admiralty Secretariat Proceedings.
ADM 36/10528 Muster Table, H.M. Sloop *Orestes*.
ADM 51/4278 Commander's Log, H.M. Sloop *Orestes*.
CUST 61/6 Custom House Letter Book, Cowes
HCA 1/25 Callendar Of Prisoners, Charges, Written Evidence & Order For Execution.
HCA 1/61 Trial Summary.
HCA 1/85 Statement of Committal.

National Maritime Museum:

2.898 BOX44 Drawings, H.M. Sloop *Orestes*.
ADM L/N70 First Lieutenant's Log, H.M. Sloop *Orestes*.

Isle of Wight Record Offices:

Burial Register 1784.
Various Baptism, Marriage & Death Certificates Relating To The Sarmon Family.

Dorset County Record Office:

Christchurch Parish Register.
Chrishchurch Poor Rate Book.

Christchurch Civic Offices:

Corporation Minutes.

Red House Museum, Christchurch:

Various Deeds Relating To Properties In Christchurch.

Contemporary Secondary Sources.

Salisbury and Winchester Journal and Hampshire Chronicle (Published Winchester):

26/7/1784
2/8/1784
16/8/1784
27/6/1785
30/1/1786

Salisbury and Winchester Journal and General Advertiser
(Published Salisbury):
   19/7/1784
   26/7/1784
   27/6/1785
   30/1/1786

Maps:
   Survey of the South Coast of England, Lt. Murdoch Mackenzie, 1785.
   Map of Hampshire, Faden, 1791.
   Chart of Isle of Wight and Spithead, Brethren of Trinity House, 1797.

Various unpublished sources in the Reading Room of the National Maritime Museum:
   Sea Officers List 1660–1815, Pitcairn-Jones.
   Ships of the Royal Navy, N.M.M.
   List of Officers of the Royal Navy, Rupert Jones.

Various unpublished Manuscripts Held at the Maritime Museum, Cowes.

Bibliography of Published Material

Archibald, E. H. H.: *The Fighting Ship in the Royal Navy*, Poole, 1987.

Arnold-Foster, D.: *At War with the Smugglers*, London, 1970.

Beaton, R.: *Naval and Military Memoirs of Great Britain 1727–1783, Vol. 4*, London, 1804.

Colledge, J.: *Ships of the Royal Navy*, London.

Gooch, E. H.: *A History of Cowes, Isle of Wight*, Spalding, 1946.

Gutteridge, R.: *Dorset Smugglers*, Sherborne, 1984.

Laird-Clowes, M.: *History of the Royal Navy*, London, 1893.

Lavery, B.: *Arming and Fitting of English Ships of War 1600–1815*, London.

Lever, D.: *Young Sea Officer's Sheet Anchor*, London, 1808.

Marshall: *Royal Naval Biography*, London, 1832.

May, W. E.: *The Boats of Men of War*, N.M.M., 1974.

Merle Chaksfield, K.: *Smuggling Days*, Christchurch, 1966.

Morley, G.: *Smugglers in Hampshire and Dorset 1700 to 1850*, Newbury, 1983.

Naval Chronicle, various articles, Vol. 1, Jan–June 1799, London, 1799.

Naval Chronicle, various articles, Vol. 3, Jan–July 1800, London, 1800.

Powell, M. F. and J. E. Clark: *Trade and Smuggling in Christchurch*, Christchurch, 1982.

Russell Oakley, E.: *Smugglers of Christchurch, Bourne Heath and the New Forest*, London, 1944.

White, A.: *18th Century Smuggling in Christchurch*, Christchurch, 1973.